The Hilton Assignment

Patrick Seale and Maureen McConville

THE HILTON ASSIGNMENT

PRAEGER PUBLISHERS
New York · Washington

Published in the United States of America in 1973
by Praeger Publishers, Inc.
111 Fourth Avenue, New York, N.Y. 10003

© 1973 in London, England, by Algonian Limited

All rights reserved

Library of Congress Catalog Card Number: 73-9393

Printed in the United States of America

Contents

Foreword

This is a true story, or at least as true as we have been able to ascertain. It is an account of a clandestine operation, mounted by European mercenaries in 1970-71 against Colonel Qadhafi and the revolutionary regime of Libya, which had to run the gauntlet of the British, Italian and American secret services. It is based on inside sources and on research at the scenes of the action in Europe and North Africa. Unlike other episodes in the continuing story of international violence, this one can be published because the chief participants were individuals acting on their own initiative and not bound by the code of secrecy which seals the lips of government agents.

Some of the names in the following pages are real; others for reasons which will readily be understood are *noms de guerre*.

London
February 1973

PATRICK SEALE
MAUREEN McCONVILLE

1 The Target

On the desert side of the North African port of Tripoli stands an Italian-built fortress dating from the 1930s. It is Libya's main jail. There, since the morning of his putsch on 1 September 1969, the young dictator Colonel Qadhafi has kept bottled up the more dangerous of his opponents. In a country not noted for the quality of its hotels, it is widely known as the 'Hilton'.

It is as austere as a Libyan smile. Its thirteen-foot dun-coloured walls, topped by barbed wire, ring a complex of cells, guardrooms and exercise yards. Two armoured scout cars guard the gate from inside where they watch over Libya's motley population of traffic offenders, criminals and, in a separate compound, 150 political prisoners.

This was the target.

Knightsbridge is not a district of London where life begins noticeably early in the morning. At seven o'clock the houses are blank and curtained, the expensive shops shuttered, the traffic still relatively light. On 28 July 1970 only a few office cleaners were about when a short, chunky South African about fifty years old parked his Buick in a street behind Knightsbridge underground station, and emerged warily into Sloane Street.

Steve Reynolds had chosen this unlikely hour for a business appointment, and that morning his behaviour was as unconventional as his timing. Arriving early, he lurked in a nearby doorway until the man he had come to meet unlocked the outer door of number 22, then slipped in furtively behind him.

The South African was up to his neck in international intrigue, a situation in which he rather fancied himself: for Reynolds was a man who liked his business adventurous and his adventures profitable. Reynolds had seen action in his time. He had spent over twenty years at sea, ending up as an officer after a long career on the lower decks. On leaving the navy in the mid-1960s he had turned freelance mariner in the Mediterranean, carrying assorted cargoes from Port Said to Piraeus, from Alexandria to Beirut, and becoming familiar with the harbours and islands of the area. This venture came to a watery end when his small freighter was wrecked in a squall off Egypt. Reynolds moved further west.

Libya was then witnessing the greatest oil boom the world has ever seen. Wells were being sunk, phenomenal strikes made and giant pipelines thrust across the desert with a speed and boldness to out-Texas Texas. Between 1961 and 1968 five major oil ports were carved out of the Libyan coast—on average, one every fifteen months. It was like the opening up of the American West. The furious pace sucked in engineers, builders, traders of every sort, and lone fortune hunters. Reynolds got a job with a contracting company and was soon making money and Arab contacts.

For the newly rich Libyans, as well as for foreign oil workers and entrepreneurs, Rome was a favoured playground, a weekend refuge from the rigours of pioneering in Libya, a place to get a decent meal, put on a clean suit, ogle the girls. A great many well-to-do Arabs come to Europe, many of them the émigré products of one revolutionary coup or another, and like migrating birds they tend to move in patterns. Where they settle often depends on historic and linguistic links, so that Paris is the magnet for French-speaking Algerians and Lebanese, London for Egyptians, Arabs from the Gulf, and anyone in search of medical treatment. Iraqis have a predilection for Austria, Syrians for Germany. The richest prefer Switzerland. But for Libyans Italy has always been the obvious place to go.

A surprising amount of Arab politics is conducted outside the Arab world. As well as the émigrés, all nursing their special grievance, there are in Europe unnumbered plotting students, quasi-diplomats on special missions, terrorists with diplomatic passports, each group with its swarm of intelligence agents watching their targets and one another. In every European city there are 'Arab' patronised blocks of service flats, 'Arab' hotels, 'Arab' places of rendez-vous. Arabs are regularly to be found in certain London gaming clubs, in the Café Frégate at Geneva, and, in Rome, at such places as the Diplomat on the Via Taro, a street in a solidly respectable looking residential area (with, incidentally, the highest fascist vote in Rome) where many Arab embassies, including the Libyan, are located. Until its closure in April 1972, this nightclub, run by a Palestinian, was the haunt of a lively assortment of Arab diplomats, businessmen and exiles, and the scene of many a surreptitious deal.

Since 1970 Rome has become the espionage capital of Europe, a title previously accorded at different times to Lisbon, Berlin, Vienna and Geneva. Apart from amateurs, many professional networks—Arab, Israeli, Western, Communist—operating in the Middle East and the Balkans are now run from Rome, which offers some foreign countries the bonus of two embassies each, one accredited to Italy, another to the Vatican, twice the normal cover for cadre intelligence officers.

It was on the fringe of this busy market in secrets and clandestine plotting that, in May 1970, Steve Reynolds heard of a coup d'état in the making. A Lebanese acquaintance told him that a group of wealthy Libyan exiles were on the lookout for military help and advice.

Eight months earlier, on 1 September 1969, Libya had been rudely wrenched from its free enterprise paradise. A fiery 28-year-old lieutenant, Muammar al-Qadhafi, had toppled the aged King Muhammad Idris in a bloodless coup, and seized power in Tripoli to the greater glory of the Arab revolutionary cause. The world of the developers and profiteers had been shattered and many of the foreigners had lost their jobs.

Qadhafi had shut down British and American military bases, was in the process of expelling the large Italian community, and showed every sign of using Libya's fabulous oil wealth to spread his fanatical brand of Islamic nationalism. He was clearly a troublemaker whose disappearance from the scene of international affairs many people would welcome—not least the rich Westernised Libyans he had driven into exile or jailed.

In Rome Reynolds had stumbled on a group of exiles determined to remove Qadhafi, but requiring assistance to do it. Not one to let an opportunity slip, he promptly let it be known through his Arab contacts that he was available for consultation. In due course he was introduced to the Libyans, and after several cautious exploratory meetings, learned of their bold plan. The Arabs wanted to make a lightning hit and run raid against an objective in Tripoli. They wanted to buy arms and military equipment, and to hire a team of European mercenaries to do the job. Was it possible? And how much would it cost?

To Reynolds this audacious proposal seemed just up his street. He imagined no great problem in mustering a private army, and persuaded the Arabs that he could make the arrangements for them. Doing some rough calculations, he eventually came up with a bizarrely precise figure of 173,000 dollars to cover all the expenses of the enterprise, a figure which the exiles accepted in principle. With the first instalment in his pocket Reynolds then set about combing the European underground for suitable contacts.

In Luxembourg he tracked down an acquaintance who had flown arms to Biafra in the Nigerian civil war. This man undertook to provide the necessary weapons. Now Reynolds was in London to recruit a mercenary team.

Numbers 21 and 22 Sloane Street, since demolished in the redevelopment of Knightsbridge, were at the time of Reynolds's visit the headquarters of the Second World War hero Colonel David Stirling. Number 21 housed Stirling himself and the offices of his small film distribution company, Television International Enterprises Ltd. Next door was the operational centre of his commercial military machine, Watchguard. Also in number 22 were the offices of James Kent, a former professional intelligence officer whose taste for action had brought him into informal association with Stirling. With their knowledge of the devious ways of secret services and governments, and with access to highly trained manpower, the two men ran the nearest thing in England to a private army and intelligence service. The houses in which they worked were linked by an internal communicating door. A well-bred girl with a cashmere-and-pearls accent manned the switchboard.

It was Kent whom Reynolds had arranged to see at seven o'clock that morning. Following Kent up the stairs to his office, he handed him a brightly coloured plastic visiting card which listed a number of obscure decorations and distinctions and a West End accommodation address. Then he bluntly got down to business. Where could he find a fighting force for a special operation against Colonel Qadhafi of Libya? The operation was political, not criminal. There was no Communist involvement. He had backers, amply provided with funds. Kent probed his visitor's story and learned of the ring of exiles in Rome, the undertaking Reynolds had given them, and the contacts he had already made in Europe. As if to confirm his claims, Reynolds pushed across Kent's desk a small roll of fifty-dollar bills. Had he come to the right address? Could he count on Kent? Might Colonel Stirling be interested?

Kent was unimpressed by a sum covering little more than a few air fares. The weather-beaten, tough-looking, tight-mouthed South African, the edge of his accent just blunted by travel, seemed an odd sort of client. His cloak-and-dagger arrival in Sloane Street, his insistence on an absurdly early meeting, the bulge of a pistol in a shoulder-holster suggested a dangerously fanciful approach to secret operations.

But however wild Reynolds's account and unconventional his appearance, Kent's interest was fired. Here was a daring enterprise which, if it succeeded, could change the balance of power in the Mediterranean and throughout the Middle East—in the West's favour. It was certainly worth considering. Kent promised Reynolds an answer in five days' time. Meanwhile he would consult David Stirling.

2 The Contract

Undoubtedly it could be done.

Reynolds's Arab backers had outlined the task with stark precision. The European mercenaries were wanted for just one night's work, a surprise assault on the main Tripoli jail, the breaching of its walls, the release and arming of its prisoners. This achieved, the visitors were to vanish as abruptly as they had come, leaving the Arabs to sort things out among themselves. The overthrow of Qadhafi, the mess and confusion of the actual seizure of power, were to be left to the Libyans. In fact the European assault force was to deliver only a component of a coup d'état, not the fully thought out, neatly packaged and securely tied up coup itself.

The clear-cut limits to the assignments were its attraction. Of course there were risks, but risks which could be calculated. This was not an open-ended mission whose success or failure depended on uncertain local politics. Instead, it was a short, sharp, in-and-out operation which could be appraised in strictly military terms.

It was straightforward; it had the element of

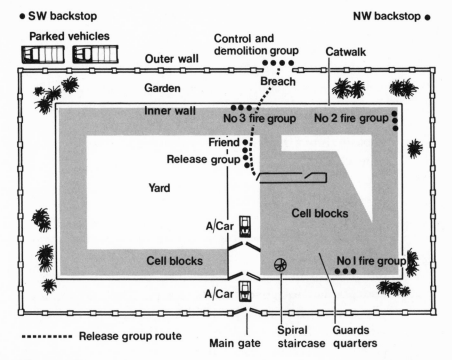

The assault teams on target

surprise; it could be carried out by a small hard-hitting force of twenty to twenty-five men who, unless things went badly awry, need never take on Qadhafi's army. It had the further advantage that the logistical build-up could take place at the European end, with a minimum of Libyan involvement.

The 'Hilton assignment' was an eminently feasible job. This was Kent's immediate assessment. Within twenty-four hours of Reynolds's visit, he was on a plane to Scotland to talk to Stirling who, he believed, would find the proposal as intriguing as he did himself.

David Stirling and James Kent share a philosophy of activism. They believe in the exercise of the individual will, in the capacity of the resolute and courageous man to shape not only his own destiny but that of nations. In their view, 'private initiatives,' independent of governments, are justified in war and diplomacy; not only justified but at times positively necessary. International politics are too important to be left to professional politicians.

The world in which we live provides such men with plenty of scope. All over the globe the established order is today threatened by subversion, terrorism, internal upheaval. Rulers afflicted with political jitters can make good use of independent experts in security and intelligence, professionals like Stirling and Kent who offer a level of expertise not locally available. If countries hire agronomists and engineers from abroad, why not safety?

The prime commodity Colonel Stirling's Watch-guard offered for sale to uneasy heads of state was a sophisticated counter-coup capability. The theory was that if a king, president or prime minister could hold out for the first vital few hours of an attempted coup, he stood a good chance of survival. To improve the odds, Stirling's experts provided an anti-coup drill, which involved a bodyguard force trained to give immediate protection against assassination; the setting up of emergency headquarters to which the threatened leader could retire in good order; and the establishment of an independent communications network through which he could reassert control.

In most countries it is politically desirable for the head of state to be seen to be protected by his own people. Watchguard, then, was not in business to provide praetorian guards. It sold training, not troops. Founded in 1967, it had quickly shown its muscle in several troubled areas of the world. Its clients were mainly African and Middle Eastern rulers. The presidents of both Zambia and Sierra Leone, for example, could sleep more soundly after Stirling's experts had tuned up palace security forces. The rich but fragile shaikhdoms of the Persian Gulf were offered similar services to fill the gap left by Britain's withdrawal. A Watchguard officer gave military advice to Saudi-financed Yemenis engaged in guerrilla operations against the Marxist regime in Aden. In this under-cover way Stirling did brisk business.

His commitment to 'private initiatives' had romantic antecedents, dating back to the darkest years of the Second World War when the 25-year-old David Stirling, then a lieutenant, was recovering in a British military hospital in Egypt from a routine brush with death. To prove that airborne commandos

could be useful in the desert war against Rommel, he
had, without previous parachute experience,
volunteered to jump from an unsuitable aircraft and
had damaged his back. Sentenced to weeks of
inactivity in a hospital bed, Stirling conceived his
master idea: that a handful of daring men could
inflict damage on the enemy out of all proportion to
their number. He had a vision of a dozen Scarlet
Pimpernels materialising out of thin air, striking
savagely, and melting into the limitless desert.

On the surge of this inspiration he gatecrashed
British Middle East headquarters (on crutches),
steamrollered his plan through the ranks of military
bureaucrats and came out with approval to train his
own sixty-strong outfit, designated L Detachment of
the Special Air Services Brigade. There was no
brigade, no air services, special or otherwise; there
was only, under this important sounding title, a tiny
private army led by a wild young officer dedicated to
blowing things up. Stirling, who had some artistic
ability, designed his own cap badge—a winged dagger
with underneath the words 'Who Dares Wins.'

For fifteen months until his capture by the
Germans in January 1943, Stirling blew things up
with resounding success. A jeep-load of men would
travel through the desert by night deep behind the
enemy lines, smuggle themselves into German air-
fields on foot and place explosive charges on parked
aircraft, then withdraw to a safe distance and enjoy
the fireworks. All in all, Stirling's SAS destroyed over
250 German planes, blasted ammunition depots and
petrol dumps, derailed trains and drew reckless rings
round the bewildered enemy. Rommel's troops called

him 'the Phantom Major' while Montgomery's verdict was, 'The boy Stirling is mad. Quite, quite mad. However in war there is often a place for mad people.'

Fervently convinced of the virtue of the lone fighter, Stirling believed he had made a contribution to the waging of modern war. The future was to prove him right. Disbanded in 1945, the SAS was revived five years later, and it exists to this day as a super-tough regiment of the British army, serving in the trouble spots of the world. Stirling never returned to the SAS but, as an inspiration and a father-figure he remained on good terms with its officers and was later able to recruit battle-hardened ex-SAS personnel for some of his peacetime 'private initiatives.'

Right-thinking Britain has repeatedly thrown up hell-raisers like Stirling, blest with cunning and courage and with the social confidence to flout the values of the worthy. When Britain was building her empire such men were heroes. In war their daredevilry was at a premium. But what opportunities for glory and self-fulfilment could a drab postwar world offer? Only, it would appear, those opportunities which one seized for oneself.

James Kent was not on the Watchguard payroll. He was his own master, an independent operator who had started life as a regular British army officer but had left the army in the 1950s to move into more subtle and less conventional kinds of conflict, largely in the Middle East. A man of above average height, he still had the soldierly straightness and the tidy mind of a staff officer. What was unusual was the gambler's courage, protected by a highly developed intuition. Stirling's career since the war had been largely in Africa, but as the focus of his interests shifted in the late 1960s to the oil-rich but unstable Middle East, he could increasingly rely on Kent's knowledge of Arab politics. Together the two men had handled a number of contracts.

Was Reynolds's proposal to be one of these?

When Kent told him of the Hilton assignment Stirling was not precisely in fighting form. A bad car crash three weeks earlier had put him in Stirling Royal Infirmary. Although only just off the danger list, he reacted favourably: this was an exploit to kindle his imagination, a daring strike quite in the old Stirling desert war manner, and on the same desert terrain.

From a technical point of view, Watchguard could do it with its eyes closed, signing up SAS veterans with fighting skills acquired in the service of the British Crown, while putting its own staff to work on perfecting the military plan. But Watchguard's working principle was to help its clients help themselves rather than to do their fighting for them. It was not in business to rent out strike forces.

There was another equally serious objection. Watchguard was a limited company, registered in Guernsey, which advertised its wares in sales literature distributed to potential customers. Although publicity-shy, it was not a clandestine organisation. To graft a wholly undercover politico-military operation on to such an overt outfit would be both difficult and undesirable—like trying to use a division of General Motors to break the economic boycott of

Rhodesia: no doubt an executive or someone in the loading bay might be persuaded to co-operate, but the company structure could not be mobilised for such a purpose. The special task needs a special organisation.

Stirling agreed with Kent that as a recognised security agency Watchguard could not touch Reynolds's proposal. But the deal was too tempting to pass up, the prize too great; for behind the Hilton assignment lay mastery over Libya's vast black underground oil-lakes, and oil business is usually good business.

If Watchguard were ruled out, its resources were not. A couple of its staff planners could be detached for the job, its mercenary contacts put to use. Stirling himself, too colourful and well-known to be officially in charge, might nevertheless serve as patron, adviser, inspirer.

To run a successful brothel in Marseilles you need a friendly policeman. On the same principle, you need the tolerance of those international gendarmes, the secret services of the great powers, to mount a military operation across an international sea against a foreign head of state. Both Kent and Stirling knew that an enterprise such as was contemplated could not hope to escape the vigilance of Britain's Secret Intelligence Service and America's Central Intelligence Agency. Unless two governments benevolently looked the other way there was little chance of success.

A fact of life of all non-official military bodies is that they cannot operate, or even begin to exist, without the knowledge and tacit approval of their

own government. Governments have to keep watch
on men and organisations active in the sensitive areas
of security and intelligence because they are a source
of power, and therefore of trouble. If they are too
troublesome, official tolerance wears thin and they
are stamped on. But they can be useful. In some
'unclear situations' governments welcome a demon-
strably private force which they can trust and if
necessary direct, while at the same time disclaiming
all responsibility for its activities.

There are occasions when situations need to be
given a push in the right direction but when overt
intervention may be hard to justify, either morally or
politically. The use of regular troops is ruled out;
even for a few weeks men cannot be detached from
the armed services to be sent covertly across a
frontier into situations of risk. What happens if they
are killed? What becomes of their pensions and
dependants? There is always someone to ask awkward
questions and blow the operation. Every now and
then all governments have a use for soldiers whose
existence they can deny. But private armies are
messy, difficult to control, usually troublesome to
the bureaucrats. It is in the uneasy narrow span
between an official nod and an official frown that
independent activists like Stirling and Kent have to
operate.

Appraising the Libyan operation therefore involved
taking the temperature in Whitehall and Washington,
nosing out what support there might be for Qadhafi
in official circles and generally gauging the scope for a
private initiative. In making these soundings, the
blunt approach was to be avoided as it infringed a

ground rule of the gentleman mercenary: never to embarrass his home government. Formal clearance was too much to hope for, and the official view had to be established without asking direct questions, or too many questions; for if they knew too much, the authorities would be driven into taking a stand one way or another. In such a situation the individual has to use political nous to determine for himself the extent of his freedom of action.

With excellent contacts in high places Stirling was in a position to test the official climate. In fact not only was he adept at sensing the trend of official thinking, but he had more than once proved to be way ahead of it. Several times he had moved into negotiation for a promising contract only to have it snatched away by the British government.

When President Jomo Kenyatta of Kenya wanted more protection in the middle 1960s, Watchguard was nearly signed up but lost the job to the SAS. In 1968 Stirling had quickly grasped that Shaikh Zayid, ruler of the wealthy little Persian Gulf state of Abu Dhabi, would be shopping around for protection. After the shaikh, with full retinue, had been to shoot grouse and stalk deer at the Stirling family estate in Scotland, David Stirling and James Kent visited Abu Dhabi to talk security. But the British government considered the defence of the shaikhdom too important to leave to a private concern like Watchguard. Similarly when Stirling offered to help the Arabian Sultan of Muscat fight off the threat from Marxist rebels in the province of Dhofar, Whitehall judged the stakes too high and again sent in the SAS.

All these were situations where Stirling and his

friends in Whitehall saw eye to eye about what
needed to be done, but in which his little agency had
been elbowed out of the picture by the official
government arm.

Stirling's American contacts were not as close, but
they existed. One of his ambitions had been to sell a
variation of his Watchguard concept to the CIA; to
persuade Washington of its need for a non-
governmental enterprise able to mount non-
attributable operations in sensitive areas. Surely, he
had argued, South East Asia, and Central and Latin
America provided cross-frontier situations which on
occasion the United States might like to have
developed? Though it played with the idea, the CIA
was not enchanted with it. Perhaps it had acquired
too much scar tissue running Cuban mercenaries
against Castro. It had learned the hard way the
drawbacks of co-operating with outsiders and engag-
ing in operations which it did not entirely control.
But the Americans kept in touch with Stirling.

What scope for a private initiative did Libya offer?
This time at least it seemed certain to Stirling and
Kent that they would face no official competition
from Britain or America. By giving up their bases in
Libya the Western powers had missed their opportunity for armed intervention, but in any event for a
government to strike openly at Qadhafi would mean
political suicide in the whole Arab world.

On the other hand it seemed equally clear that
Qadhafi was no favourite of the West. From the
moment of his emergence he had aroused in official
circles the same gut reaction of suspicion and distaste
which had greeted the young Nasser seventeen years

earlier. Qadhafi was evidently a Nasser Mark II, outbidding his master in xenophobia and political extremism. He was already squeezing the oil companies and the likelihood was that he would use every dollar in his bulging bank account to sabotage Western positions. Any day now the Russians might jump into the vacuum created by his irresponsible gesturing. To cut the upstart Qadhafi down to size in one clean, swift, discreet and essentially non-attributable strike should win nothing but applause.

Hearteningly there was reason to suppose that Whitehall would turn a benign blind eye on the escapade. An incident which had occurred two months earlier now fell into place.

On 18 May 1970 a retired high-ranking British official had called at 21 Sloane Street for a general chat about the political situation in the Middle East. He had served in Libya and it therefore seemed quite natural that he should turn the conversation to Qadhafi. In his opinion the September 1969 coup was a scandalous development which all right-thinking people must be anxious to do something about. It was a disaster for Britain, no less for America and the other Western powers, and particularly for Western oil interests.

The three men agreed to give the matter further thought. At a second, a third and then a fourth follow-up meeting at different Pall Mall clubs over the next month, Kent and the former official exchanged the information they had collected and discussed the prospects for an insurrection against Qadhafi. The ranks of Libyan exiles were combed through for someone rich, prominent and motivated enough to lead the movement. A short list of six men was prepared.

When the South African Steve Reynolds visited Sloane Street a few weeks later, looking for a strike force, Kent and Stirling were already well briefed on Qadhafi and his enemies. The intriguing touch was that the Arab whom Reynolds had met in Rome, the millionaire exile in search of mercenaries, was none other than the prominent Libyan whom they had already identified as the most likely coup-leader, the man at the top of their list.

His name was Umar al-Shalhi.

3 The Principal

Outside Geneva in an expensive, well-guarded villa within a mile of the French frontier lives the man who lost Libya to Qadhafi.

Umar al-Shalhi and his brothers had been like sons to King Muhammad Idris. No one was closer to Idris or more trusted by him. No one in the kingdom enjoyed such power at court or in the country. For half a century the Shalhi family had served the Sanussi as advisers, lieutenants and courtiers-in-chief, and in the shadow of the throne had come to hold the substance of power. If Idris was the sovereign, they were the state. The Shalhis were not of noble lineage, they were not members of one of the great North African tribes; but their long and faithful service to the ruling family had given them as much claim as anyone to run the nomad-populated desert which was Libya.

Childless himself, King Idris brought up the three Shalhi brothers at court, sent them abroad to be educated, groomed them for unrivalled authority at his side. In a still primitive society where the shaikh was master of all resources, it was natural for the shaikh's 'adopted sons' to consider these resources as their inheritance. For years the Shalhis ran the country like a family business, making and breaking premiers, allocating contracts, disposing of oil revenues, moving into the multi-millionaire bracket on Libya's fantastic surge of wealth.

And then, in a few hours before dawn on 1 September 1969, an unknown army officer stripped the powerful Shalhis of their patrimony. With a handful of soldiers Qadhafi ended the Sanussi reign, sweeping King Idris, his favourites and the whole structure of his power into oblivion. Deposed, Umar al-Shalhi vowed to bring down the usurper and to restore if possible his sovereign, so reclaiming his own rightful position. In all the world the young Libyan revolutionary had no more bitter opponent than the exile brooding in his Geneva villa.

Estimates of the fortune which Shalhi had amassed during Libya's years of prosperity in the 1960s range from twenty-five million dollars upwards. A large part of this wealth, safe from confiscation in foreign banks, now helped take some of the sting out of his predicament. He was ready to devote his last dollar and his life to fulfil his 'sacred duty' to King Idris, but meanwhile he lived well in his Swiss haven.

The house stood in its own grounds, had garage space for several cars, a swimming pool, accommodation for servants and a separate suite of rooms which was Shalhi's own den. His wife, mother and sister lived elsewhere in the house. A high wall protected by electronic devices enclosed this small estate. Further security was provided by a number of Sudanese bodyguards who doubled as house servants,

Umar al-Shalhi (Associated Press)

drivers, and cook. His secretary, a man, was a thickset
Egyptian. In addition to this elaborate household
Shalhi had an office in central Geneva, an apartment
in Vienna with a panoramic view over the Danube,
and a luxury flat looked after by an Italian cook-
housekeeper in London's West End.

At thirty-six years of age Shalhi looked ten years
older. He was a short, bullet-headed man built like a
tank, his powerful torso thickened with the sort of
solid fat which makes for strength rather than flab.
His hair was cropped so short that his head looked
shaven. Framed by an equally close-clipped grey
beard, his face betrayed some of the impatient
arrogance of a man used to having his way and not
given to restraining his temper. His left hand was
misshapen.

Riding in his Mercedes or driving his silver-grey
Maserati, wearing handmade crocodile leather shoes
and well-cut Italian suits, his tie held in place by a
large black pearl stick-pin, he looked like an opulent
Arabian princeling. But Shalhi was far more than a
playboy. He had good taste, a quick intelligence,
reserves of will to drive himself as well as his
subordinates into sustained effort, and above all a
flair for the Byzantine intrigue of Arab power
politics. He had, after all, grown up at court. These
gifts were now to be put to the test.

Would they put him back where he belonged? How
to do it? How to turn the clock back to before the
first of September? What cards could he still play in
Libya? These were the questions which devoured his
waking hours—and which led to another nagging
query: where had he gone wrong? In his key position

at the king's side, how had he failed to spot the threat
from Qadhafi? Why had his informers and the secret
police let him down? Had someone—the Americans?—
betrayed him?

Shalhi was not cut out for a government job.
Unlike his father and his two brothers, he was not
happy in office, preferring to move the levers behind
the scenes and make money as a businessman. Too
impatient for the routine boredom of an official post,
even at the top, with highly developed tastes for
expensive European pleasure, he was a man who
sought power without responsibility. Because he was
a Shalhi he got it. In Idris's regime he had wielded
immense influence but had been accountable for
nothing.

What allowed him to get away with it was an
accident of history and geography. For a generation
Libya had been a sheltered area, a country only
minutes of flying time from Europe yet almost as
isolated as Tibet. It is less a country than a desert,
one of the world's greatest and most barren.

Half the size of India, two and a half times the size
of Texas, seven times the size of the British Isles, it
has just about enough people to fill one large city.
There are today fewer than two million Libyans
thinly scattered over 700,000 square miles, most of
them living on the narrow coastal strip between the
desolate wastes of the Sahara and the Mediterranean
sea, the rest roaming with their camels from one
remote oasis to another. Twenty years ago it was one
of the poorest countries in the world: ninety-four per
cent of its people were illiterate; the infant mortality
rate was a horrifying forty per cent; per capita

income was forty dollars a year; and only a dozen Libyans had graduated from university.

The only thing of value Libya had to offer was strategic advantage to outsiders. No European power—or for that matter world power—could ignore that its 1,200 miles of coastline and the vast emptiness of its interior made the country a natural base for the command of the entire Mediterranean.

It was this strategic importance which set the powers squabbling over the future of Libya after the war. The Russians suggested they look after it, Egypt wanted to annex it, the French said it should be carved up between themselves, the British and the Italians. The British were willing to share it with the French but thought it a mistake to bring back the Italian colonists who, from 1911 to their defeat in 1943, had not exactly made themselves loved in Libya. The Americans favoured handing it over to United Nations trusteeship for a decade.

As compromise was impossible the UN cut the Gordian knot by making Libya independent in 1951—the fifth independent country in Africa, after Ethiopia, Liberia, South Africa and Egypt. Britain and America were well content because they already had what they wanted. As victors of the war against Germany they were firmly *in situ*. With the British in Cyrenaica—the navy at Tobruk and the RAF at El Adem—Whitehall was assured of alternative Middle East bases in the event of the evacuation of the Suez Canal zone. Meanwhile in Tripolitania to the west, the United States was spending 100 million dollars to develop Wheelus Field into one of the largest air bases outside America and a key link in its Cold War chain

King Idris (Associated Press)

encircling the Communist bloc. Wheelus grew into a
self-contained American township ringed by a ten-
mile wall and offering its six thousand inhabitants
about the only luxuries available in Libya, and its
airmen near perfect facilities: immense desert space
to fly in, no people to get in the way of bombing
practice, no reparations to pay, and a clear blue sky
360 days of the year.

With Britain and America so powerfully present
and the Libyans so pitifully weak, the country was
shielded through much of the 1950s and 1960s from
the violent·growing pains of Arab nationalism. One
after another Arab countries were crumbling under
the blast of Nasser's activism. In Iraq the monarchy
was overthrown; Syria tumbled into union with
Cairo; the Yemen was torn apart by civil war; Jordan
staggered from crisis to crisis. Just next door to the
source of all the excitement, Libya escaped, allowing
men like Umar al-Shalhi to prosper undisturbed.

He benefited from another, this time purely local,
umbrella, that provided by Muhammad Idris
al-Sanussi, King of Libya, spiritual father of the
nation, forty-fourth descendant of the Prophet
Muhammad.

For forty years Umar's father, Ibrahim al-Shalhi,
had been Idris's most devoted companion. He had
joined Idris in 1916 when the young prince, then in
his mid-twenties, had just taken over leadership of the
Sanussiya, an unusual family enterprise. Founded by
Idris's grandfather and greatly expanded by his
father, it was an Islamic missionary society preaching
a return to the fundamentals of the Koran from a
chain of religious foundations stretching from Yemen

to Algeria. In the days before frontiers and nation states in the Arab world the Sanussiya was a powerful political force in North Africa as well as a religious one. At the height of its power in the 1880s, under Idris's father al-Mahdi, the order had perhaps two million members eagerly spreading the message of puritan reform.

The Sanussi family were remarkably long-lived, spanning almost two hundred years in three generations. Born in Algeria in the 1780s, Muhammad bin Ali, the Grand Sanussi, was a pious intellectual who after years of missionary journeys deep into Arabia turned back for home across the Sahara about 1840. But as the French had taken over Algeria in his absence, he was forced to settle in Cyrenaica which thus became the centre of his movement. By the nomads who fell under his spell the Grand Sanussi and, after his death in 1859, his son al-Mahdi came to be regarded as the overlords of all the desert shaikhs, and as such defended their people first against the Turks and later the land-grabbing Europeans. This warrior role came to them all the more readily because their religious fundamentalism gave pride of place to *jihad*, the holy war against the infidel.

In his turn Idris inspired resistance to the Italian invaders when Mussolini in the 1920s ruthlessly brought the whole of Libya under his control. Idris was driven into exile in Cairo for twenty-two years before his return home in triumph in 1944. He had been shrewd enough to believe throughout the war in an Allied victory and was rewarded when Britain backed his candidature for the throne of newly independent Libya in 1951. At his side through all these ups and downs was Ibrahim al-Shalhi serving as confidant, adviser and Controller of the Royal Household. Shalhi's authority was second only to the king's.

In October 1954 this valued friend and servant was murdered in a Benghazi street by a nineteen-year-old Sanussi prince from a collateral branch of the family. The motive was dynastic. Idris had no children and determined that on his death the succession should pass to his brother or his brother's son. This inflamed those cousins who held Shalhi responsible for barring their way to the throne. More loyal to his friend than to his family, Idris had the assassin put to death (and his body exhibited on the spot where Shalhi had fallen), banished a conspiracy of other princes to a distant oasis, swore to cherish Ibrahim al-Shalhi's sons, and promptly appointed the eldest, Busairi, as his chief adviser.

The Shalhi dynasty seemed as securely established as that of Idris himself. They led the field of a dozen families, most of them linked with the great tribes of the interior, who formed the ruling oligarchy, providing as circumstances required prime ministers, police chiefs, officers of state. As the king grew older, frailer, more preoccupied with religion and more remote, the men he had chosen ruled unchallenged.

This game of political musical chairs could, it seemed, have gone on indefinitely, with the players occasionally swapping portfolios and the policies remaining the same. The king rarely intervened except to keep in balance the various centres of local power—Tripoli versus Benghazi, the police versus the army, one tribe versus another. For the rest of the world Libya was a country easy to forget. What income it had was derived from renting bases to Britain and America, from the sale of modest quantities of barley and dates—and of scrap metal collected from the debris of war in the desert.

Then came oil. Gushing from the timeless desert in an ever-swelling flood, it shattered for ever this poor peaceful backwater. In the ten years from the discovery of oil in 1959 to Qadhafi's coup in 1969, Libya was transformed from one of the poorest countries in the world to one of the richest, from one of the most insignificant to one of the most dynamic in Arab and Mediterranean politics.

It was the fastest and biggest boom in history. Libya seemed to float on a limitless sea of oil. The galloping production figures had to be revised as soon as they were put on paper. In one decade forty-one foreign companies sank 2,500 million dollars in exploring, exploiting and exporting this black and viscous wealth across the water to Europe, the most thirsty market in the world. By 1969 Libya had elbowed past most oil producing countries and seemed to be heading for third place behind the United States and Venezuela. A country which had been getting by on under ten million dollars a year suddenly found itself struggling to spend hundreds, and then thousands of millions.

No society could stand up to such a battering of riches, certainly not one so primitive and unprepared as Libya. For a few years the cracks in the social and political structure were camouflaged by the king's own modest life and the unchanged pattern of the court. But there were rumblings. It was in 1964 that

Libya began to emerge from its sheltered area into the storm.

In March that year Idris, the father of the nation, announced his intention to abdicate. Behind this stunning news lay a palace tiff, a conflict between a young new prime minister and his aged sovereign. Responsive to Arab nationalist feeling which at long last had crossed the sand buffer between Egypt and Libya, the prime minister told Washington and London that they would have to pack up their bases when the leases expired in 1971 and 1973. Ever loyal to the British, the king was aghast, and shut himself up in Tobruk until crowds of tribesmen, as well as ministers, senators and deputies flocked to his palace to beg him not to abdicate.

A month later Idris suffered a second blow. His closest adviser and Court Chamberlain Busairi al-Shalhi, son of his old companion Ibrahim, was killed at the wheel of his Ferrari.

Busairi had been an able, if ruthless, official, a king-pin of the king's power system, cleverly playing off the British against the Egyptians to keep Libya's oil flow undisturbed, but not altogether trusted by either. He had married an Englishwoman, Eve Pinnock, daughter of a civil servant, but he was generally regarded as anti-British, perhaps because of unhappy experiences at Exeter University, England where he had studied in the early 1950s and where he met his future wife. After his death his English widow married one of his brothers, a not uncommon practice in the Arab world. Her new husband was Abd al-Aziz al-Shalhi who had graduated from military school and provided the military under-pinning for the family fortunes.

For the first time for half a century there was no Shalhi officially at the king's side. Umar, the third brother, did not covet Busairi's job. He had better things to do. Instead of accompanying Idris from one austere and uncomfortable palace to another, he wanted to be where the money and the action were, in the main stream of the flood of oil and contracts. He ignored the warning signals.

The Arab defeat in 1967 brought the Russians into Egypt in strength, and it was against this peril to the east that Libya's Western advisers moved to protect her—and their own interests. Libya climbed another rung of the ladder of international importance when in 1968 she was talked into buying from Britain three hundred million dollars-worth of sophisticated air defence, including surface-to-air missiles, radar and communications equipment. As it happened Lieutenant Colonel Abd al-Aziz al-Shalhi was head of the armed services' supply committee as well as Director of Operations, and as such the man who, at considerable profit, tied up this gigantic deal.

The people of Libya, and the junior army officers, were not oblivious to what was going on. The vast scale of the transactions, contrasted with the still widespread poverty in the country, could not be overlooked. Nor could the soaring cost of living. Moreover many young Libyans were learning to be indignant that their country was still shamefully tied to Western apron strings and had not sprung to Egypt's defence in the war against Israel.

Nearing his eightieth birthday, King Idris felt events slipping from his grasp. He missed his Shalhi.

In April 1969, five years to the day from Busairi's fatal car crash, Umar al-Shalhi, the playboy businessman, took formal office as Royal Counsellor.

It was a fateful move. Fawned on by foreign contractors, envied by other Libyan businessmen less fortunately placed than himself, despised and feared by the tribes, he was not a popular man. Many saw him as chief profiteer, the man who diverted into his own pocket the wealth that was rightfully theirs.

What frightened his enemies was that Umar al-Shalhi appeared, with the king's backing, to be digging himself in on a long-term basis. As if to lend his favourite legitimacy the king early in 1969 ordained that Umar marry the seventeen-year-old daughter of Hussain Maziq, a former premier and head of the powerful Barasa tribe. She was already engaged, but the king insisted, and the marriage took place. But a tribal alliance calculated to give Shalhi respectability and support earned him nothing but bitter resentment.

The crux of the Libyan problem was that no one could see the monarchy surviving the death of Idris, who in his own way was profoundly respected not only for his piety but for his discreet political skills. He had named as his heir his nephew Prince Hasan al-Ridha, a mild, shy, middle-aged man totally un-equipped for the job. Clearly power was going to be up for grabs.

The Shalhis had long since perfected their plans, not so much for a coup d''etat as for the 'preserva-tion' of their own highly privileged status. Their assets included Abd al-Aziz's hold over the Cyrenai-can Defence Force, an armed militia outnumbering the army; friends controlling the police; a private army of informers in shops, offices and the homes of well-placed foreigners; and, or so they supposed, the backing of the Western powers. Above all they could draw on almost unlimited funds to buy off or silence a critic or a rival. Like everyone else the Shalhis took it for granted that no one would make a move so long as the king remained on the throne. If he died or abdicated, it was another question.

In the summer of 1969 there were rumours at the Libyan court that the king, tiring of the burden of responsibility, might abdicate in the autumn after his holidays in Turkey and Greece. As Royal Counsellor and to be close to his master at this important time, Umar al-Shalhi travelled abroad with King Idris, Queen Fatima and their suite in July and August. At the same time his brother Lieutenant-Colonel Abd al-Aziz decided to send off for training in England forty young officers who, his spies told him, had been voicing criticism of the regime.

The stage seemed set for a smooth transition to a new regime, with the Shalhis still on top. But at two a.m. on the morning of Monday 1 September 1969, twenty-eight-year-old Lieutenant Qadhafi upset this carefully scripted scenario.

News of the coup reached King Idris and Shalhi at breakfast time at their hotel at Bursa in north-west Turkey on the Sea of Marmara. Deeply hurt by the humiliation of not stage-managing his own exit, Idris turned down a suggestion from the new masters of Tripoli that he should abdicate and return home as an 'honoured citizen.' Instead he made his way first to Greece and later to familiar Cairo where Nasser gave him asylum.

But Umar al-Shalhi was not ready for retirement. Twenty-four hours after Qadhafi's coup he was in London, pressing Michael Stewart, the Foreign Secretary, to use force to restore Britain's old friend Idris. The minister, said a Foreign Office spokesman, 'did most of the listening.' Shalhi flew on to New York, but was dissuaded from proceeding to Washington by the stony reception of the American administration. The message in both Britain and America was that overt intervention against the revolutionary regime from Western bases in Libya was not practical. It was out of date, it was not politic.

If an overt strike against Qadhafi was ruled out, what about a covert one? This was the question Shalhi took with him into exile.

4 Heir Non-Apparent

In a country as vast and sparsely settled as Libya the key to the seizure of power is communications. Control the switchboard and 700,000 square miles are yours. On the eve of his coup Qadhafi was a lieutenant in the Signals Corps in Libya's British-trained army of under ten thousand men. As a promising young officer he had been sent to England in 1966 on a ten-month army signals course at Beaconsfield, and probably knew as much about the mysteries of radio transmission and reception as anyone else in Libya. It was a skill which helped him to the top.

Although fired by zeal for the Arab cause from his schooldays, it was only as a 21-year-old officer cadet in 1963 that he began actively to plan for revolution. With a handful of classmates he formed in 1964 his secret society of 'Free Unionist Officers' which rules today. In the six years it took him to realise his dream, Qadhafi kept the conspiracy alive by maintaining constant contact with his former classmates. They were scattered in lonely army outposts deep in the Fezzan and on the desert frontiers with Chad,

Algeria and the Sudan. Even the two principal garrisons at Tripoli and Benghazi were seven hundred miles apart. The way he did it was by radio, encoding his message in a simple cypher invented by himself. He sat at the centre of the web.

To be sure of success the conspirators had to take over the country's main power centres—the army and police barracks, the three broadcasting stations, the ports and the royal palaces. This meant striking simultaneously at both Tripoli and Benghazi, as well as at the king's own newly built city, Al Baidha. For months they watched for the moment when all members of the government would be in one place, all top-ranking army officers in the country, and the king well away from his loyal stronghold, Cyrenaica. Zero hour was changed and changed again. Only good communications could cope with these reversals.

In the planned triple strike, the most difficult target was Benghazi, base of the Cyrenaican Defence Force, the main prop of the Sanussi throne. Like King Faisal's White Guard in Saudi Arabia, the CDF was conceived as a counterweight to the regular army, and Idris spared no pains to insulate it from the political contamination of urban Arab nationalists. The CDF was a paramilitary body of Saharan tribesmen equipped with armoured vehicles, helicopters and light artillery. When the regular army wanted Chieftain tanks from Britain, the king insisted his praetorian guard be supplied with anti-tank weapons. It was his counter-coup capability and Watchguard would have been proud of it.

In the western wing of his kingdom Idris kept his army in check by matching it against the equally well-armed Tripolitania Police.

On the night of the coup Qadhafi made it his own business to neutralise the dangerous CDF. His men arrested the force's commander-in-chief at Barce on the Cyrenaican coast and compelled him at gunpoint to call in his principal officers by radio telephone to an urgent meeting. As they arrived they were arrested, and Qadhafi then swept down on Benghazi capturing its post office, radio station and governorate virtually unopposed. Once again it was his command of army communications which had opened the door to success.

Meanwhile his fellow conspirators were carrying out carefully timed assaults in Tripoli and Al Baidha. Within twenty-four hours both the CDF and the Tripolitania Police had been stripped not only of their officers, but also of their weapons, ammunition dumps and tanks. The signals lieutenant and his Free Unionist Officers were in sole command and the cream of Idris's regime was in the 'Hilton'. No blood was let. It was one of the neatest jobs in political surgery which the Arab world had seen in years.

In accordance with his instincts Qadhafi installed his Revolutionary Command Council in the news room of the Libyan radio and television offices, a new building on the sea outside the centre of Tripoli. For some days nobody knew who the new masters were, or even where they were, but stories about their youth, idealism and informality began to filter out and gradually a picture emerged of twelve young men, all under thirty, red-eyed and unshaven after night-long debates round a table piled high with state papers and machine guns. Perhaps trembling at the

enormity of what they had done and at the size of
the prize in their hands, they kept their heads down,
concealing their identities as best they could and
threatening 'severe punishment' for anyone pub-
lishing their pictures.

The Arab states were as baffled as the rest of the
world. On the morrow of the coup delegations from
half-a-dozen Arab capitals, each suspicious of the
others, rushed to Tripoli to discover who was behind
it. Was Qadhafi a Marxist? Was he a Baathist, of the
Syrian or of the Iraqi persuasion? Was he the
instrument of the Beirut-based Arab Nationalist
Movement led by George Habash then making the
running among the Palestinian guerrillas? Had he
seized power with Saudi money or Egyptian intrigue?
Was he a British stooge or a creature of President
Pompidou's Mediterranean policy? Had he been
'Made in USA' by the Central Intelligence Agency?
No Arab, at least, could believe that the Libyans had
overthrown Idris on their own and unaided.

The international press took a full week to put a
name to Libya's new leader—and then uncertainly.
Wrestling with the problems of Arabic transliteration
journalists came up with a dozen variations:

Moamer al Kozafi (*The Times*, 9 September 1969)
Omar Moammer Kazzafi (*International Herald
Tribune*, 9 September)
Moammer El Kadhafi (*Corriere della Sera*, 9
September)
Maamer el Kadhari (*Guardian*, 9 September)
Moammer el Kadhafi (*Le Monde*, 10 September)
Muammer Gaddafi (*The Observer*, 13 September)
Moamer al-Kazafi (*New York Times*, 15 December)

Muammar el Qaddafi (*Sunday Times*, 11 January 1970)

etc, etc.

Only in the third week of September could outsiders give this baffling name a face, when Qadhafi appeared in public in a brand new uniform with lots of gold braid on his cap, over-shadowing his still scruffy entourage. The chairman appeared to have charisma, a good command of classical Arabic and the unnerving, horizon-scanning eye of a visionary. Very little more was known about him.

The date and exact place of his birth are unsure. He was born in a goatskin tent somewhere in the Sirtica, the great wilderness which divides northern Libya and today provides the country with most of its oil. Some say the date was 1940, some 1942, but his birth went unrecorded. What is certain is that Qadhafi was the child of humble folk who earned a meagre living growing a little barley and raising livestock: a life his parents and three sisters still lead.

The first lesson Muammar al-Qadhafi learned was the wickedness of the Italian colonisers. He was born too late to experience effective Italian rule himself, but his grandfather had been killed in the invasion of 1911, and between the two world wars both his father and uncle fought in the Sanussi resistance, were captured by the Italians, condemned to death and reprieved. The camp-fire epics of Qadhafi's childhood were all about the heroic deeds of the tribesmen and the atrocities of their conquerors: Mussolini's aircraft bombed the oases in the 1920s, long before the bombardment of civilians raised world outcry in the Spanish civil war.

It was a lesson in nationalism. At school it was to sink deeper and take on a wider significance until it filled his whole horizon.

Qadhafi was a bright lad, and his father scraped and borrowed to send him first to a Koranic school at Sirte on the coast, and then to secondary school deep inland at Sabha, the capital of Fezzan. He went on to study history and geography at Benghazi University, but transferred to the military academy at the end of his second year without taking a degree. For the child of a nomadic tribe in a largely illiterate country, he had what amounted to a privileged schooling, but what really formed his mind was the radio.

He grew up with a radio, tuned to Cairo, jammed into one ear and with the other listening to the great silence of the desert. It would be hard to overrate the formative effect of Cairo's 'Voice of the Arabs' on countless youngsters of Qadhafi's generation. Started in 1953 and beamed to the whole Arab world, it was a violent, scurrilous, clever, myth-making instrument of Nasser's rising power which worked to destroy all opposition to him and mobilise the Arab peoples behind his leadership. But it forged its listeners into a single, self-conscious community, inflamed by ancient memories of Arab glory and hopes for vengeance against the West and its creation, Israel. A 'Voice of the Arabs' broadcast was heady stuff:

> Dear Arab brothers, raise your heads from the imperialist boots, for the era of tyranny is past! Raise the heads that are bowed in Iraq, in Jordan and on the frontiers of Palestine. Raise your head my brother in North Africa. The sun of freedom is rising over Egypt and the whole of the Nile valley

Colonel Qadhafi (Associated Press)

will soon be flooded by its rays. Raise your heads
to the skies!

The teenaged Qadhafi raised his head from his
school-books and saw his vision. He had been weaned
as a Libyan nationalist; he now became an Arab
nationalist. Night after night he and his classmates sat
in the desert at Sabha dreaming of Nasser and of the
destruction of Israel which they believed he could
bring about. For them even more than for the young
of Britain, the Suez war of 1956 was a watershed.
The rumours that Libyan air bases had been used in
the British attack on Egypt aroused them to fury.
Next to Allah and his Prophet, Nasser was the most
sacred thing they knew, and from then on Idris, who
gave succour and military bases to the allies of their
enemy, lost their loyalty. Graven on every Arab heart
are the three dates 1948, 1956, 1967—three Arab
defeats at the hands of Israel, each deepening the
sense of shame and feeding the fires of revenge. Such
was the background of Qadhafi's education.

A second powerful force in the moulding of his
mind was Islam, not the urbane, watered down Islam
of our day, but the narrow, militant brand forged in
the desert by the Sanussi family he was to overthrow.
When still a schoolboy Qadhafi swore an oath to
practise his religion, to say the prescribed prayers and
forgo the proscribed evils of alcohol and loose living.
He is as zealous as he is pious. There is a striking
similarity between his fundamentalist missionary
outlook on life and that of the Grand Sanussi,
Muhammad bin Ali, defender of the faith in the
1840s. For both, the Koran and the Tradition of the
Prophet were alone acceptable as sources of law and

doctrine. Both became revolutionaries when their puritan reformism, confronting secular enemies, was forced into political channels.

In the 1970s Qadhafi is an anachronism, brooding on the Arabs' imperial past and preaching a return to the uncompromising purity of seventh century Islam. It is probably true to say that such a man could emerge in modern times only in the heartland of Arabia or in the great deserts of the Sahara, sheltered areas immune for generations from the virus of Western civilisation.

Once a dictator—or a company chairman—is in office, the job begins to look as if it were made to his measurements. Power confers its own authority, puffing up the most improbable candidates into larger-than-life figures whose unremarkable past is easily forgotten. The weeks and months before Qadhafi's seizure of power were rich in trivial incidents and accidents which could have robbed him of the prize, leaving him an obscure lieutenant without a future, or dead.

The Free Officers originally planned their coup for early 1969. Qadhafi in Benghazi set the ball rolling in January with a four-line letter to his principal lieutenant Abd al-Salam Jallud (carried to Tripoli by a sergeant in the Signals Corps), ordering him to check the plotters' hold over troops, vehicles, weapons and ammunition. This satisfactorily done, zero hour was fixed for 12 March.

Then came the first setback. The conspirators learned that a recital was to be given that night by the idol of the Arab world, Umm Kalthum. Matronly, middle-aged, given to singing songs for hours on end,

she is more a force of nature than a performer, whose
hold over audiences from the Atlantic to the Persian
Gulf is incomparably greater than that of any pop
star in the West: it used to be said of her that of all
Arabs she alone could overthrow the late President
Nasser. With this deity in town, the revolution did
not have a chance. Most of the wanted men on the
conspirators' list would be at the concert, and since
the singer would be warbling on into the early hours,
it would be impossible to arrest them without
sounding a general alarm. In any event it seemed bad
form to the young officers to carry out their takeover
under the cover of the revered Umm Kalthum.

In the nick of time the coup was called off, and
instead of marching on Benghazi Qadhafi dropped in
on his family at Sirte. His troubles were not over.
Driving back to camp at midnight he and two other
officers lost themselves in the desert and spent the
rest of the night looking for the road. They had
scarcely found it when a puncture overturned the car
into the ditch. It was a critical moment. The
complete blueprint for the postponed coup was in the
wreckage and liable to be discovered. In fact the only
embarrassing discovery made by their rescuers was a
bottle of distilled water which was taken for gin. The
puritan young man who had never touched alcohol in
his life had to endure a diatribe against drunken
driving. There and then he vowed to ban liquor once
his revolution triumphed.

Zero hour was rescheduled for 24 March, but again
had to be put off when King Idris made an
unexpected visit to Benghazi. It was then set for 5
June, but by this time the Shalhis' suspicions had

been aroused. Several Free Officers were suddenly switched to new jobs, others were sent abroad on courses, and the blueprint had to be redrawn.

Throughout all these vicissitudes Qadhafi's officers were haunted by the fear that, with the aging Idris close to abdication or natural death, they might be forestalled by the Shalhis. Rumours reached them that Lieutenant Colonel Abd al-Aziz al-Shalhi had, of his own initiative, issued ammunition to an armoured unit and posted it to the main barracks in Tripoli. Other senior officers in Shalhi's circle were sleeping at ammunition depots, and military intelligence was mounting a round-the-clock watch on barracks. It was reasonable to expect the Shalhis to strike the moment the king announced his abdication. When Idris, with Umar al-Shalhi at his elbow, went abroad that summer, Qadhafi could postpone his coup no longer.

Qadhafi was to tell the Libyans that he had not overthrown King Idris so that Libya could become 'an ordinary republic like any other republic.' In fact it was soon clear how very unusual a republic Libya was going to be. The minimum wage was doubled and ministers' salaries halved. All rents were cut by thirty per cent. Alcohol, that evil of all Western evils, was banned, and the multi-million dollar business of liquor importing ended. Roman script disappeared by administrative decree, taking with it the neon from the streets, the 'no parking' signs and the Pepsi-Cola bottles—until their labels could be reprinted. All official correspondence, all form-filling, even menus and hotel registrations, had to be made out in Arabic and dated from the year of Muhammad's Hijira in 622 AD rather than from Jesus Christ. English was struck

off the primary school syllabus. Revolver in hand the
self-promoted Colonel Qadhafi led a posse of policemen to shut down the Bowlerina night-club in Tripoli
which had dared import dancing girls. Barclays DCO,
the biggest bank in the country, was first renamed
Bank al-Jumhurriya ('Bank of the Republic') and
then taken over. A handful of Jews and some thirty
thousand Italians were expelled, their property
confiscated in 'holy revenge' for their iniquities
against the Arabs. The cathedral of the Sacred Heart
of Jesus, symbol of Catholic colonialist Europe in the
heart of Tripoli, was sanctified as the mosque of
Jamal Abd al-Nasser, and the Libyan fire brigade
given the daunting task of removing the crosses
dominating the city skyline from the dome and
bell-tower.

Altogether it was a reactionary, xenophobic, fun-
hating clamp-down.

Within days of the coup the young Cromwells who
made all these radical changes moved from the radio
building to the greater security of the Aziziya
barracks in Tripoli. They lived and worked behind
three perimeters bristling with machine guns and were
rarely seen in public. The founder members of
Qadhafi's Revolutionary Command Council were
bound by ties of almost superstitious loyalty to each
other, appearing to believe that they stood or fell
together and that their rule would last as long as they
were united. In the search for unanimity the all-
night-long sessions continued.

They lived modestly in army quarters, as they had
before the coup, disposing of the fleet of six hundred
Mercedes Benz which King Idris had bought for his

officials and officers. The RCC preferred Volks-wagens, small Fiats or, better still, army landrovers. Scandalised, they put on show for journalists the silver mess-kit, the television sets, the ornamental pistols and solid gold Beretta which these schoolboy revolutionaries had found in Idris's palaces. The palaces themselves were turned into boarding schools, hospital annexes and homes for delinquents.

Like a guerrilla leader Qadhafi lived with his men. At short notice in the middle of the night, he would summon foreign ambassadors to his office in the barracks, a bare, comfortless room decorated only with framed texts from the Koran and a battery of telephones. His private life was, and remains, mysteri-ous in the extreme. All the public has been told is that he divorced his first wife Fathia, a bride found him by his mother, and on coming to power married Wasfia, a nurse. Nasser was best man at the wedding. A typical, self-effacing Muslim wife, Wasfia stays at home inside the military compound and is not talked about.

To Umar al Shalhi, Qadhafi is a usurper issued from the barrel of a gun. Shalhi seeks restoration in the name of the Sanussi, founders of modern Libya; in the name of his own family, servants of the throne for more than half a century; in the cause of secular, Western-style progress.

Qadhafi sees himself as the custodian not only of Nasser's legacy but of the message of the Prophet Muhammad as well, the herald of a second golden age of Arab power.

5 The Team

On 9 August 1970 Steve Reynolds checked into the small hotel at Bridge of Allan, close by Keir. He had flown from London to Scotland that morning to meet Stirling. Things had moved fast since his call at Sloane Street two weeks earlier, and he had been told that subject to certain important conditions the operation was on. He had reported to Shalhi in Geneva that there was in London an organisation with the resources, capability and high-level contacts to provide the fighting force they wanted. Now he was in Scotland to discuss the military, political and security implications of the assault.

Keir's baronial setting was calculated to impress and reassure the South African. Here the Stirlings, a Lowland Scottish family of landed gentry, had lived for generations. David's father was a brigadier-general and his mother a daughter of the 13th Baron Lovat. The family home, where in his elder brother's absence David was now convalescing, was a spacious country-house built amid formal gardens round an inner court and set in rolling farmland. The estates included large tracts of moor and forest where young Stirlings

learned to shoot and fish. An ancestor who found the
sight of servants and tenants approaching the house
offensive had dug a gully to the back door.

Reynolds liked what he saw. The atmosphere of
land-owning, near feudal privilege, no less than the
charming giant who received him, convinced him that
the Libyan affair was in good hands. Stirling at
fifty-four was a striking figure, 6 foot 5½ inches tall
and slightly stooped as if in apology for his height. To
Reynolds it seemed that the legendary Stirling had
only to pick up the telephone for a task force of
desert commandos to materialise, toasted into action
by the mandarins of Whitehall. Here was confirma-
tion of the mix of military expertise and political
underpinning which the operation needed.

But Stirling was still a very sick man. Had he been
wearing a safety belt at the time of his accident, he
would surely and instantly have been killed, for the
crash flattened the roof of the car to the level of the
radiator. As it was, only his unusually strong
physique had pulled him through, and it was going to
be a long time before he was fit again for full-time
work.

When Kent flew to Scotland on the day after his
first meeting with Reynolds, he had two objectives.
The first was to secure Stirling's agreement in
principle to being associated with the operation. For
all his individualism Stirling was a loyal member of
the establishment whose military arts were not for
sale to each and every customer. Mere gold had never
been his motive. His inclination was to fight for the
established order of legitimate rulers against the
agents of violent change. His loyalties were to the

democratic, liberal, Christian West, and particularly to Britain and the British legacy abroad.

An audacious, cross-Mediterranean strike against Qadhafi fitted not only Stirling's principles of warfare, but also his political morality. Qadhafi was clearly a menace. It was time he was removed.

Kent's second objective was to persuade Stirling that the Libyan operation would have to be run entirely separately from Watchguard, with all overt links severed. A wholly covert headquarters would have to be set up.

Both points had been satisfactorily settled on July 29, and now with Reynolds it was agreed to time the attack on the 'Hilton' for mid-September, one month ahead. Speed would be a guarantee against leaks or traitors, but it meant packing a lot into the month. Reynolds left for London well content with progress.

Kent now set about establishing a secret London base. He rented for six weeks a small furnished house in Montpelier Street, Knightsbridge, and, close by, opposite Harrods, a large apartment in a big block conveniently equipped with several elevators and entrances. Montpelier Street was the command post in which Stirling, slowly recuperating from his accident, was installed to lie low. He was put in the care of a young former SAS officer recruited to help with communications, run the house, do the shopping and generally look after the Colonel. The apartment opposite Harrods was to be the general headquarters used for contacts and briefings. These arrangements were not cheap but they were more secure than hotel suites.

Clandestine, but not criminal. This was Kent's

inflexible rule. He was determined there should be no illegality in the preparations for the strike. Everyone had to be able to make overt and confident use of telephones, hotels, air transport, and all the other facilities of modern living. There should be no such childish nonsense as false beards and false passports. The arms and equipment had to be legally acquired. If the plan collapsed at any stage there must be no comeback.

Drafted into the secret headquarters were two of Stirling's military specialists, John Brooke Miller who had retired early from being a Regular Army officer and Jeff Thompson, an ex-warrant officer with eighteen years of British army experience. Small, spare, made of whipcord and wire, his clothes, hair and face all the same even light tan, Thompson was a west countryman in his late thirties who was a good deal tougher and more ruthless than his quiet manner suggested. Not easily rattled, he was just the sort of man needed for the Hilton assignment. In the army he had seen active service in Aden, where he formed a low opinion of Arabs, and in the Far East. He had done a training contract in Africa for Watchguard, but was not a permanent member of it: detaching him from the overt organisation presented no problem.

Miller had more permanent connections with Watchguard which were not so easy to conceal. He took a month's holiday and under this cover was seconded to Montpelier Street. Miller had been an acting major in the SAS and was well looked on by Stirling. In his early thirties, he was a good-looking young man, well-spoken, socially acceptable and abrasively sure of himself. Militarily he was less sure, but he had qualities of dogged determination and was a painstaking staff officer.

Thompson and Miller made a good pair.

Intensive planning began in August. The Arab principal had laid down a clear objective, the prison in which were locked up not only his own brother Abd al-Aziz but over a hundred senior army and police officers as well as the leading politicians and senior civil servants of King Idris's regime. Umar wanted these key men freed and armed for action against Qadhafi. How this was to be done he left to his European friends.

Should the assault be made by land, sea or air? The easiest solution was to infiltrate the team into Libya in ones and twos, by car overland from Tunisia or by scheduled flights, posing as businessmen and oil workers. They could then meet at a desert rendezvous and be supplied with weapons by air drop. Or the men themselves could be dropped by parachute. Reynolds knew where he could pick up a DC6 aircraft flown by mercenaries during the Biafra war and still available for adventures. But the planners had little confidence in this suggestion (and, as it turned out, with reason: a few weeks later the aircraft developed engine trouble on a substandard airstrip in Central Africa and it was thought cheaper to leave it to rot than to salvage it).

The gap in all these plans was how to get the men away if things went wrong; it would be distinctly unpleasant being a foreign mercenary in Libya after a failed coup. To win the team's support, any plan had to include fail-safe provisions for bringing them home. Helicopters were considered an obvious vehicle for this sort of commando strike, but were ruled out for lack of a base in a neighbouring country. They were also thought too vulnerable to ground fire and had a record of operational unreliability.

The group in Montpelier Street spent long hours debating the merits of each of these alternatives. They ended by discarding them all. Their aim was to keep it a watertight operation, in and out, independent of the ultimate success or failure of the coup against Qadhafi. This clear, uncomplicated objective was what had attracted Kent and Stirling in the first place. And so, because Tripoli was conveniently situated on the coast, a decision was made in favour of a sea attack. A small worry was the four British-built fast patrol boats recently delivered to the Libyan navy, and its only craft. But Shalhi's contacts in Tripoli reported that two of the vessels were out of action for want of spares, and as for the rest, the officers of the Libyan navy were not among Qadhafi's staunchest admirers and could possibly be bought off.

Eventually the planners boiled down the assignment to a four-line proposition: assemble a British team in Glasgow; move it to Malta; from there embark for a seaborne landing near Tripoli on the Libyan coast using landingcraft operating from a mothercraft.

Already Jeff Thompson and John Miller were recruiting the team, though without revealing what they would be used for. They were looking for men between the ages of twenty-five and forty, tough self-reliant former soldiers who could handle all types of small arms and had been trained to kill; preferably men who had seen service in the commandos or the Parachute Regiment. They had to be old enough to know the business, tough enough to have survived in it, and unimaginative enough still to be taking orders. One or two would have to know about explosives. In practice they were predominantly ex-SAS.

It is news to no one that the Special Air Services' name is a disguise to hide its real function. It is not an air regiment although its men can be dropped by parachute if necessary. It is primarily a penetration unit trained to operate on the ground behind enemy lines, to destroy, to create confusion and collect military intelligence. It specialises in working close up front in sensitive political situations. Although it exists as a permanent regiment, its men are recruited from other units on secondment for periods usually of three years, and are selected only after a gruelling physical test. All this contributes to the prestige and the *esprit de corps* of the force. But what do such men do when they retire still young, tough and fit from the army?

The team was contacted by word of mouth, the standard mercenary way of recruitment, made all the more feasible this time because so small a force was required, no more than a couple of dozen. Twenty-five determined men are often more effective than a hundred, because in a force of a hundred at least half are busy training or supplying themselves or the other half, instead of getting down to fighting.

Sorting out likely candidates was a very personal affair. Ex-soldiers with their own reasons for wanting to get away from civilian life tend to know each other's records. Going through the list of possibles,

Thompson or Miller would red-pencil a name: 'You remember so-and-so? We can't have him!' And they would go back to some incident, a lapse in action or a brawl in a bar, when the man in question had become bad news.

Of the men who were good news, one worked in a garage, another had his own shop, a third ran a pub which his wife took over when he was away, a fourth was a barman, a fifth had a smallholding. One was a surveyor who could fit in the operation with his holidays, though whether he came back from his holidays was another matter. There are in the world plenty of restless people, people who take to adventure because life is boring, who choose to row the Atlantic or fight other men's wars. If they have acquired military skills, they can more easily find an outlet for such energies. An attraction of the Hilton assignment was that the whole thing would take only a few days, there and back. So short an absence posed few family problems for any of the men. There was no question of lengthy training or five-mile runs; this was a job that required hard men, not super-fitness.

Essentially it was a job for men with clean records. It was absolutely vital that they were not in trouble with the police and that their passports were valid. They had to be able to move out of the country and cross frontiers without hindrance. Criminals were out. There was no room for men on the run. One ex-soldier, Thompson discovered, was suitable for the job, except that he had obtained a passport fraudulently. He had paid £25 to a farm labourer who had never even left his county let alone Britain, for the use of his name and other formalities, details which he sent in on the application form together with his own photograph and an accommodation address. Back came a valid passport. But when Kent heard of this the man was dropped from the team.

The only really useful mercenary is a hungry mercenary. Mostly mercenaries operate for loot, but in this assignment none was foreseen and anyone who stayed to loot would probably not come back. The final payment was the substitute for loot, 5,000 dollars a man, quite an attractive proposition for a night's work. The men expected the going rate for soldiers plus a sizeable bonus, enough to last a few months and for some to finance a real bender. From the planners' point of view it was important to get the level right: not too low to exclude the professionals, not so high that it would attract the 007s.

When they were taken on the men were given a down payment, but not such a handsome sum as to arouse outsider interest. The last thing the planners wanted was for a member of the team to live it up at this stage and give the game away. But there had to be some front money. Some of the men had been short-changed on previous jobs. They wanted to know the money promised them this time would be forthcoming.

So that was how it was. The word had been put around and the men recruited. Now the planners in Knightsbridge found themselves with a force at their disposal which could take on the best in the land.

No one pretended to the team that there was not a high risk element in the operation. Men with the initiative and self-reliance to be mercenaries are not idiots. More than the average man they know what foreign conditions are like, they weigh risks, make judgments. They would only risk their necks if convinced that what they were being paid to do was worth doing and that the chances of success were considerably better than even. Above all they had to believe in the efficiency of the outfit which recruited them, and in its leadership.

One Saturday afternoon in late August 1970 the twenty-five members of the team made their way singly to the apartment opposite Harrods for a morale-boosting pep talk from the Colonel. The handsome drawing room which held all of them without crowding was quiet, but underneath the casual surface was a current of excitement. Stirling, still very unwell, was able to muster the strength to make a brief charismatic appearance.

Then John Brooke Miller as the team leader and Jeff Thompson as his number two briefed the team. They were told they had been engaged for a short, sharp, hard-hitting job abroad lasting from start to finish about two weeks. They were not told the country concerned nor the target to be attacked. They were not encouraged to ask questions. On being given the signal they were to proceed to an assembly point in Glasgow where they would be instructed on their next move. For each there was 5,000 dollars already deposited on account. It would be released to them after the operation and if they did well, there would be more, much more . . .

6 Reconaissance

It fell to John Brooke Miller and Jeff Thompson to prepare the detailed military plan for the assault on the Hilton, a minute by minute drill from before landing to re-embarkation. Shalhi's intelligence had supplied a report on the prison together with a rough sketch map drawn by a former prisoner showing the layout of the buildings, the approach roads, the well-guarded main gate. But several vital features were missing which only on the spot reconnaissance could fill in. How many and how vigilant were the sentries on the walls? How often was the guard changed? Where would the explosive charges have to be placed and how thick were the walls they would have to breach? In August, while Kent was busy with administration in London and Thompson was finalising recruitment of the team, Miller and Reynolds flew to Tripoli in the guise of businessmen to take a long hard look at the target.

If this was the lion's den, the beast appeared to have had its teeth and claws drawn. Tripoli in high summer seemed sunk in sleep. Few people were about in the sun-drenched streets and in this young military

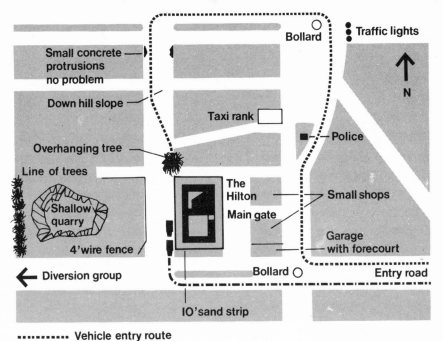

Small concrete protrusions no problem

Down hill slope

Overhanging tree

Line of trees

Shallow quarry

4' wire fence

Diversion group

Bollard

Traffic lights

N

Taxi rank

Police

The Hilton

Small shops

Main gate

Garage with forecourt

Bollard

Entry road

10' sand strip

.... **Vehicle entry route**

—·—·—·— **Vehicle exit route**

Street plan of the Hilton area

dictatorship there were few uniforms to be seen, save for one or two traffic policemen sweating in the thin shade of the palm trees fringing the harbour.

Shop after shop in the arcaded avenues of the town centre was shuttered, their Italian owners already packing their bags on orders from Qadhafi. Trade in the souk was slow and faces long. The government was not spending any money, neither were business-men. This recently prosperous Mediterranean port seemed to be slipping into a predictable and hopeless quagmire of underdevelopment. Discontent was rife, if unvoiced. To Miller the place seemed a pushover.

Reynolds rented a small apartment from which the Hilton's bleak barbed-wire topped walls could covertly be scanned through binoculars. For three days and two nights the two men observed the prison and its routine as best they could. Miller also fulfilled another important task. Ostensibly taking time off for a little sightseeing, he hired a car and spent a couple of hours exploring the beaches to the east of the town. Within fifteen miles of Tripoli he found what he was looking for, a gently sloping beach in a sheltered bay near the main coast road that would make a first-class landing place.

To provide some protection Reynolds had taken trouble to establish good relations with the Libyan authorities, beginning with an approach to the embassy in London. He had passed on to the military attaché the information that a small airline was overflying Libya on discreet trips from Luxembourg to South Africa in contravention of the boycott imposed by the Organisation of African States. The Libyans' grateful interest gave Reynolds a pretext for a visit to officials in Tripoli.

At Tripoli airport on their way home, there was an anxious moment when Reynolds was selected for a more thorough than usual security check. He was led away and searched but nothing came of it. Apparently the Libyan officials were on the look-out for illegally exported currency and the pistol hidden in his baggage was not discovered. Miller and he were soon safely off the ground, minus some self-composure but with an operational plan of the prison and its defences.

From what they had seen of the jail, the beach and the lonely. road through the dunes and derelict palm-gardens which connected them, Miller and Thompson were able to perfect the plan. Together with Kent they drew up a full list of the weapons and explosives required, from detonators and signal pistols to something big enough to stop a tank. Reynolds flew at once to Luxembourg where he had a contact in the arms trade. He told him to place a firm order with Omnipol, the Czechoslovak state arms export agency. Instructions about the time and place of delivery would be given later—at the right moment.

Shalhi in his unforthcoming way was well-pleased with developments. After a year of exile and frustration he was getting somewhere at last.

In spite of his chilly reception in London and New York in the first days after the coup, he had still hoped that Britain and America would not abandon their old friend Idris and that they would, when the world was looking the other way, quietly remove the troublesome young revolutionary. But these illusions were quick to fade. East and West soon scrambled for Qadhafi's favour, Russia recognising his regime within three days of the coup, with Britain, America, France and Italy rushing in a day later.

It was a further blow to Shalhi when, a week after Britain's recognition, Donald Maitland, Principal Private Secretary to the Foreign Secretary Michael Stewart, arrived in Libya as Britain's ambassador to the new regime. Maitland flew into Tripoli on 12 September on the first commercial flight after the airport was reopened to traffic. A small, dynamic Scot, he was a high-powered official, and his appointment suggested the importance Britain attached to the job. Speaking and writing fluent Arabic and with first-hand experience of service in Cairo and Baghdad, Maitland was a leading example of the new, post-Suez breed of British diplomatist keen to come to terms with Arab nationalism and break loose from Britain's tutelary past.

The signs were that Britain wanted as good a relationship with Qadhafi as the Colonel would allow, a discouraging thought for Shalhi and his compatriots in exile.

A surprising number of top Libyans had escaped capture by Qadhafi on 1 September, thus avoiding imprisonment in the Hilton. Driven to more temperate Europe by the rigours of the Libyan summer, they had quite literally been saved by the weather. These exiles included a clutch of former premiers and cabinet ministers, a few score courtiers and entrepreneurs and, apart from Idris himself, another member of the royal family Abdullah bin Abid, a nephew of the king usually referred to as the 'Black

Prince' (from the darkness of his features, his mother being of a Sudanese border tribe). By January 1970 several of these men had made contact in Rome to exchange news from Tripoli, appraise the situation and review their prospects for a comeback.

Rome was a natural magnet for these dispossessed Libyans. For many it was a second home and Italian a language hardly less familiar than Arabic, one of the few benefits Libyans could claim from Mussolini's interest in them. Before the revolution it was not unusual for a rich man to fly across the narrow stretch of Mediterranean for a night out on the Via Veneto. After the coup and particularly after the influx of the expelled Italian settlers, Rome was still the European city with the closest Libyan links, the listening post for picking up the latest news from home.

It was here that in February 1970 the Black Prince and a group of the more active émigrés determined to pool their resources and attempt a counter-coup. The outcome was the abortive Chad conspiracy which ended in a Libyan courtroom twelve months later.

The intention was to assemble a force of troops and weapons in the Chad capital of Fort Lamy and then shuttle them by aircraft to an airstrip in the Fezzan, the vast sunbaked wasteland of southern Libya, crossed by long valleys and dotted with oases like small islands amid a desolate sea. Once landed, the insurgents planned to arm the Fezzan tribes for a march on the north, and to broadcast news of their rebellion on the airfield's radio in the hope of sparking off an uprising in Tripoli.

Security was idiotically poor. No sooner had

emissaries from the Black Prince made contact with tribal chiefs in the Fezzan than the news was passed to the government. When the aircraft carrying an advance group landed in June Qadhafi's men were waiting. The following month the regime squeezed some propaganda mileage from the incident by announcing that the accused had confessed to being the vanguard of a 5,000-strong force of European mercenaries 'armed by the CIA,' equipped with planes, armoured cars, artillery—and poisoned daggers.

Shalhi had never had any faith in a tribal revolt. He had spent half a lifetime in the palace, his privileged place frequently assailed by tribal intrigues. He knew how fickle and corruptible the beduin leaders were. 'Raising the tribes' was an outdated myth: at worst a passport to failure, at best no more than a diversionary exercise to veil some more realistic plan. He did not believe a conspiracy'could be mounted in the desert a thousand miles from Tripoli and succeed. The first decisive blow would have to be struck in the heart of the capital itself.

His judgment was confirmed by the Chad fiasco. Meanwhile Shalhi had decided on his own plan of action. With two associates he established a secret war fund in a Swiss bank to which each contributed according to his means. Then after much careful thought they hit on the idea of an attack on the Hilton. It was beautiful in its simplicity. Judging his countrymen ineffective for such a strike, Shalhi decided that the job must be done by foreign professionals. It was at this stage in May 1970 that they made contact with Reynolds. The Hilton assignment was on offer.

To bury their tracks and protect themselves from Qadhafi's intelligence, it was agreed that they should leave Italy and disperse. Rome, their home from home, was becoming too hot. It was crawling with Libyans, many of whom had made their peace with Qadhafi or were eager to do so. They were not to be trusted.

A more actual threat came from the Egyptian intelligence service, without doubt the most effective of the Arab services, equal in sophistication, at least on Middle East affairs, to the services of the major powers. Since the 1950s Rome had been a special target for Egyptian intelligence, not only as a prominent centre of Arab émigré life, but also because it was an arena for the murderous conflict between Egyptian and Israeli secret agents. Shalhi knew that in Rome Egyptian intelligence would soon pick up his trail. Cairo had identified Qadhafi as a friend and would be eager to protect him.

International conspiracies of any magnitude require a friendly base, usually in a country neighbouring the one to be attacked. But in the case of the Hilton assignment there was none. Chad had been disqualified by failure, and anyway was separated from Tripoli by a thousand miles of Sahara. Egypt was an enemy. Little Tunisia and her sick and ageing President Bourguiba were too preoccupied with internal crises and too vulnerable to counter-attack to risk antagonising the young colonel. Algeria had little time for Qadhafi's rhetoric but was too engrossed at home to chance foreign adventures. No government,

Arab or otherwise, was prepared to provide a spring-board. The expedition had to be mounted in space.

For the English planners at their secret London headquarters this meant they would have to perform a considerable conjuring trick. The three elements of the strike—the men, the weapons and the ship to carry them to their target—would have to be brought together at the last moment, on the very eve of the assault, at a point within easy reach of Tripoli. Only in this way could they avoid detection.

Malta was geographically tailor-made for the jòb. If the British Government was prepared not to interfere, its strong British connections would be an added advantage. It was decided therefore that Malta should serve as the point of departure and return for the assault force. Kent had never been there and as there were many loose ends of planning and administration to be tied up, he took the teatime plane on 15 August 1970 to Valletta where, savouring the irony of the choice, he booked into a suite at the Malta Hilton. Reynolds was already there.

Kent started with the waterfront, looking for small hotels near the harbour where he considered the team would not feel out of place, preferably hotels run by former British soldiers who had settled in Malta. In each case he told the owners he was looking for accommodation for a ship's crew of four or five men who would be arriving some ten days hence. The idea was that the team would filter into Malta a couple of days in advance and lie low until embarkation.

Then Kent reconnoitred the coast east and north of Valletta to locate suitable beaches where casualties, should there be any, could be landed clandestinely and without fuss. He found a small private hospital run by Catholic nuns to whom he told a story about a team involved in underwater exploration off the Maltese coast. It was hazardous work, there was always a chance of something going wrong and of someone getting hurt. In case of trouble, might he in advance reserve a private ward? It was all very plausible.

Down at the harbour, Reynolds's task was to arrange the hire of a suitable vessel. He had told Kent that he had identified several possibilities and as Reynolds was a sailor by trade, Kent left it to him. But Reynolds soon ran into problems. Optimistically he had planned to take a boat on dry lease, without crew or stores, but he quickly discovered that this was not the way things were done on short-term contracts. To charter a boat for about a month required a wet lease, with captain and crew on board.

This was not a reassuring piece of information. It implied that control of a vital element in the plan, the transport of the team, would be in the hands of an unknown third party. It threatened security. Nor was Kent overjoyed at the boats Reynolds fancied, luxury yachts for the most part, not only with crew and captain but with the owner as well, chewing on a cigar in the wheelhouse. Although they had the necessary speed, these floating gin palaces were surely not what was required.

Reynolds had come to Malta with his secretary, Tracey, a tough 22-year-old English girl with a strongly developed sense of survival. Kent was disturbed to find her there. Reynolds had said in London that the girl knew nothing of their plans, yet here she

was, chatting up ships' captains and evidently in the
know. Why did Reynolds tell him one thing and do
another? The inconsistencies in Reynolds's stories
were beginning to pile up alarmingly, while in
proportion Kent's confidence in Reynolds's ability to
handle his part of the assignment dropped. But they
were stuck with him. He was the intermediary with
the Arab principal. Kent resolved to establish direct
contact with the principal as soon as possible, and
meanwhile to treat Reynolds with added caution.

Kent had planned to return to England on
Tuesday. A telephone call from Montpelier Street late
on Sunday evening caused him urgently to change his
plans. Early on Monday morning he took the first
flight back to London. The operation had run into a
difficulty potentially far more crippling than
Reynolds's whimsical choice of boat.

At the beginning Reynolds had told Kent that he
had 'cleared' the plan with the SIS and CIA. He
followed this up with further assurances, and in
support name-dropped about contacts in the British
and American intelligence services, even claiming that
the United States ambassador to London, Walter
Annenberg, had attended a meeting between himself
and CIA representatives. Kent, who knew well the
inner workings of Whitehall, was sceptical, and at the
Keir meeting with Reynolds he and Stirling refused to
mount the operation with a British team if the British
government were opposed to it. To still all doubts,
Reynolds promised that a 'senior British official,'
whom he would not name but who he said was
known personally to Kent and Stirling, would telephone them at Keir several days later. On time the

call came through, but it was from Reynolds himself to explain that clearance had been delayed a day or two for 'technical reasons,' but that all was well.

All was far from well. Independently of Reynolds, someone in the SIS had telephoned Miller at his home to warn against the use of British personnel in the assault on Qadhafi. Miller was shaken. He was still very much the ex-British army officer used to having official approval for everything he did. If the government did not like it, that was good enough for him.

But was it the government? At what level had the decision been made? Was it only an administrative ruling of bureaucrats, or was it a policy decision reached after careful consideration by ministers? How final was it?

To find the answers Stirling's contacts were mobilised. On different days he arranged at short notice a meeting with someone very senior indeed in the secret service, and then at the Foreign Office with a minister of Edward Heath's new government, Anthony Royle, a former SAS Territorial Army officer who after the general election that June had been appointed Parliamentary Under Secretary for Foreign Affairs.

Both gentlemen gave Stirling a firm no. On no account were British nationals to be sent into Tripoli.

Whitehall considered that a venture involving Stirling and ex-SAS personnel would inevitably be laid at Britain's door. Eventually the Foreign Office would have to assume responsibility for its success or failure, and either way would probably suffer from an Arab backlash. Gunboat diplomacy was not only risky, it was unfashionable. The whole trend of

British policy was to withdraw from involvement in Arab affairs, rather than to intervene more actively, and to sanction an attack on Qadhafi would mean reversing this course. No one in official circles particularly liked Qadhafi, no one disputed that he was a dangerous troublemaker; but no one had the will to bring him down.

What did the veto amount to? Had the Hilton assignment failed even before it started? Kent had never been sanguine of getting full British approval to use British personnel, at best he had expected a blind eye. As he thought the matter through, his confidence revived. Very well, the British team would be stood down. Stirling himself would of course withdraw. But there was it seemed enough distaste for Qadhafi in Whitehall for Britain to look the other way if someone else did the job, *and did it fast.*

Kent was not unprepared. Within hours he had arranged the closing of the Montpelier Street and Knightsbridge headquarters, paid off the British team, and was on his way to France to make alternative arrangements.

7 Counterplot

When James Kent entered the gilt-and-crimson lobby of the Hotel George V in Paris in the early evening of 9 September 1970, the liveried concierge handed him two telephone messages. One he was expecting—it was from Marcel Klein, the man he had come to see, and it invited him to dinner. The other read: 'A friend from Beirut is anxious to meet you. Please ring Room 2207 at eleven p.m.' This message was to add a new and dangerous dimension to the Hilton assignment, but for the moment Kent could only put it out of his mind and concentrate on Marcel.

Marcel was a little man with a Napoleonic complex, a film scriptwriter who had in his time chalked up a festival award or two but was now down on his luck. As sometimes seems to happen in France, the criminal world he depicted on the screen had spilled over into his own life, so that he had made useful friends in the milieu, brothel-keepers, bent policemen, good-time girls—and mercenaries. He did not stoop to crime himself but took advantage of knowing the right people and introducing them to each other.

For a man in the contact business Marcel had himself proved unusually hard to contact and Kent had been chasing him fruitlessly for over a month. Only a couple of hours after Reynolds first came to Sloane Street shopping for a mercenary force, Kent was dialling Marcel in Paris on the hunch that this was a job for tough French Foreign Legionnaires rather than decent Englishmen. But Marcel was not answering the telephone that afternoon—nor the next day, nor the next. By now it was August 1, the beginning of the great French annual shut-down when half the population heads for a month in the countryside or on the beaches. Like most of his countrymen Marcel had dropped out of sight.

Kent sent a young woman to Paris to pick up his trail. She checked with the concierge servicing Marcel's block of flats and with the neighbours on the floor above, but only came up with the thin news that Marcel had gone, as he did every year, to Annecy in the French Alps.

This was the one clue Kent had when he left London on August 17 in search of Marcel. He flew to Geneva, hired a car, and drove the forty miles south to Annecy across the border to make the rounds of the main hotels. He drew a blank.. At the *hôtel de ville* an obliging official checked through the *fiches*, the record of hotel guests filed daily for the French police. Still no trace. With his trail petering out, Kent had to return empty-handed to London, and it was only ten days later, when Marcel got back to Paris from his holiday (spent, it transpired, a couple of miles outside the Annecy municipal boundaries) that contact was finally made.

Hiring a private army was not the sort of business that Kent was prepared to do on the telephone. It meant another trip to France and a lunch with Marcel at which he outlined his requirement for 'twenty-five good guys' deliverable within seven days for an unspecified assignment. Marcel was confident he knew just the man to round up such a force. For a fee of 5,000 dollars he was prepared to make the introduction. Expensive? Perhaps, but he knew the French mercenary scene and its petty criminal fringe. He would be supplying not some small-time thug or mere soldier of fortune, but an experienced, reliable team leader, someone very rare and valuable, on whose skill and nerve much would depend.

After a month on the move Kent needed a breather. There was no point in drawing attention to himself until the new team was ready, so he drove south to the Riviera to spend a week in comfort at the Carlton Hotel in Cannes. He was a man who could work himself hard when necessary, but liked his world well-lined with luxury, an undercover agent who operated from suites in Europe's best hotels. There were sound practical advantages behind the luxury. The better the hotel, the greater the privacy and the reliability of its staff; the more efficient its communications and other facilities. Security is an expensive commodity.

Marcel Klein was as good as his word. When Kent met him at the Hotel George V to go out to dinner on the night of September 9, Marcel had things arranged. The team leader, a veteran mercenary named Léon, would be waiting in the *salon de thé* upstairs at Orly Airport at 9.30 next morning.

After dinner Kent took leave of Marcel. Now for his second appointment. He chose to telephone room 2207 from the relative anonymity of a café near the hotel, then settled down with a cup of coffee to wait for the friend from Beirut.

In war there are few stationary targets: seen from another perspective, the pursuer is the pursued. With a growing feeling of having been here before Kent began to trace that night the outlines of a plot which mirror-imaged the Hilton assignment. Just as Umar al-Shalhi meant to bring down Qadhafi, so it now appeared Qadhafi was gunning for Shalhi. And to get their rival jobs done both contestants had come shopping in Sloane Street.

Two men sat down at Kent's table in the café on the Avenue George V. One was his Lebanese acquaintance, Ahmad Shawkat, a financier who had a private score to settle with Shalhi: they had been to school together at Victoria College in Alexandria. Kent had heard that the CIA figured among Shawkat's many international contacts. He had last seen him in the Dorchester Hotel in London where Shawkat had introduced him to King Hussain of Jordan. In the Paris café that night Shawkat was accompanied by Yassin Ubaid, a Libyan with an office in Rome from which he operated overtly on the margin of the oil world while covertly peddling political and commercial information of a more or less sensitive nature to those who would pay.

In most major European centres such men are to be found today, entrepreneurs whose function it is to link oil-rich but still rudimentary Arab governments with Western firms eager to do business with them.

Surprisingly few Arabs know their way around commercial Europe, and equally, few Western businessmen are at home in the palaces and prime ministerial offices of the Arab world. Both need go-betweens. Inevitably politics get mixed up in the trade talks, and the intermediaries are as capable of lending a hand in putting together a *coup d''etat* as a contract. Whatever the business they earn their commission.

Angling in Tripoli for a business opening for one of his American clients, Ubaid had soon discovered that Shalhi was seen there as the most dangerous threat to the new regime. It appeared that Qadhafi did not want him assassinated, but that his dearest wish was to have Shalhi brought home in irons to be put on public trial. Nothing would so confirm Qadhafi's own legitimacy as a full-dress indictment of Idris's reign— of which Shalhi would be the symbol. Like Steve Reynolds on a similar occasion Ubaid was quick to appreciate his opportunity, and promptly offered his services to Qadhafi's secret police as an intermediary able to hire the kidnap squad they needed. When they rose to his bait, he consulted Shawkat who, he believed, had the right sort of contacts in London.

The Lebanese had telephoned Sloane Street in the first week of September, but with Stirling lying low and Kent out of the country, he had been obliged to cool his heels. London was able to tell him however of Kent's expected arrival in Paris on the ninth. Now he had come with Ubaid from Rome to put his proposal: he wanted to hire a gang of European mercenaries for a dirty night's work, to seize Shalhi one way or another and turn him over alive to the Libyans.

As a professional Kent allowed himself a moment of elation in being the man at the point of inter-section of both plot and counterplot. If he needed reassurance that he was at the heart of this particular imbroglio, this was it. But his satisfaction was tempered by the worrying second thought that the Libyans might have had wind of the Hilton assign-ment and had mounted the counterplot in order to penetrate it. Should this be the case, he was in danger indeed. On the other hand, if they had come to him unsuspectingly, the kidnapping proposal provided him with a direct line to the enemy, and the more he could learn of Qadhafi's defences, the better for Shalhi.

When Kent expressed guarded interest, Ubaid proposed a follow-up meeting in Rome at which detailed strategy could be discussed. Coolly he suggested that Kent could ask the Libyans for two million pounds sterling for the job—adding that his own commission on the deal, if it came off, would be thirty per cent. The sheer audacity and venality of the plan suggested to Kent that Ubaid at least was probably not double-crossing him. He seemed to be playing it straight for profit. Kent agreed to be in Rome on 21 September. Life was going to be complicated, running with the hare and hunting with the hounds . . .

Marcel was waiting at the foot of the escalator leading up to the departure floor at Orly when Kent arrived a moment or two before half-past nine next morning. He led Kent up to the tea lounge, sat him down at a table and made his way over to two men sitting together by the windows. He then returned with one of them, a muscular, dark-haired Frenchman in his late thirties, wearing a polo-necked sweater and a black leather jacket, whom he introduced as L'eon.

Kent liked the look of him. Léon had the quiet self-assurance and the natural good manners of the really strong. One felt he had no need to impress by fast talking or throwing his weight about. His French was slow, simple and well-articulated, and Kent, whose grasp of the language was shaky, could follow every word. His was a classic mercenary background, with French army service at Dien Bien Phu and then in Algeria in the First Parachute Division, where independence had put him into the mutinous ranks of the OAS, the settlers' terrorist army which fought to keep Algeria French. When de Gaulle put down the OAS rebellion, Léon preferred exile to jail and turned mercenary, taking on engagements in the Congo and Biafra. The 1968 amnesty for political offenders permitted this hardbitten soldier of fortune to come home to France and settle down in Paris with his new mistress Annette.

After preliminary introductions, at which Kent and Léon sized each other up, Léon called over his second-in-command, Jules, a tiny slip of a man, gay and capricious—and absolutely lethal. He was a fine foil for the stocky, cautious-moving Léon.

By the time the coffee cups were empty Kent had explained that he was looking for a well-balanced force of twenty-five men to mount a mercenary operation in a foreign state. They would be asked to ferry arms to insurgents inside the country concerned and would run the risk of clashing with local troops.

Mercenaries like other men have their ideological preferences—loyalties, fears and inhibitions deriving from their country of origin. Kent recognised this truth and, without going into too much detail, put Léon's mind at rest. First and foremost he assured the Frenchman that the operation was in no way directed against French interests anywhere in the world. Secondly, it had nothing to do with the Arab-Israeli conflict—an important qualification, because feeling runs deep in France on one side and the other of this struggle and because the underground has a healthy regard for the Israeli secret service. Thirdly and lastly, Kent specified that the operation he was planning was not aimed against the Soviet bloc. Léon's men would not be asked to engage in silly heroics along the Baltic coast or to crash the Curtain into Eastern Europe. No one would end up mining salt in a Siberian labour camp.

As an earnest· of his seriousness—and a small thank-you to the three men for having come to see him off—Kent slipped Marcel seven 100-dollar bills to be appropriately distributed between them, then went through the departure gate to board his plane for London.

In London his first call was on David Stirling who had moved to a suite at the Hyde Park Hotel for a couple of weeks' convalescence when the Montpelier Street headquarters was given up. Stirling had retired from the Hilton assignment but Kent wanted his agreement to the continued active involvement of Jeff Thompson. He also wanted to be able to call on assistance and advice from John Miller.

After the veto on the use of British personnel in

the actual assault, Miller had refused to go in with the troops and Thompson was hesitating. But their military plan was still sound. Thompson's role was now to nursemaid the French team into action and back up Kent's staff work at the London end.

It was at this point that the retired senior British official, who had come to Sloane Street in May breathing fire against Qadhafi, unexpectedly reappeared. He called on Stirling and Kent in the hotel suite overlooking Hyde Park, a visit which rose to high comedy at times, as both sides knew a good deal more than they were saying. As in May, so now their visitor was not overtly an emissary of the British government, but his radically changed attitude suggested that he too had responded to Whitehall's veto. Early in the summer his line had been that Qadhafi was an enemy and that no effort should be spared to bring him down. Now, without any reason given or acknowledgement that he had once thought otherwise, he was as fervently convinced that it was not in Britain's interest to take action in Libya. Clearly the authorities had not forgotten the Hilton assignment.

If Shalhi told you to meet him off the ten o'clock plane, you could be sure he would fly in an hour earlier or later or come by road. He had learned to be cautious. He eliminated routine from his life, and moved fast and without warning from his well-guarded Geneva base on frequent journeys across Europe. This seemingly impulsive mobility was his best protection against kidnapping or assassination.

The counterplotters, meeting in Rome on 21

September 1970, recognised they had a problem. Kent had arrived as planned for further talks with Ubaid and to learn from him everything the Libyans knew about their quarry. The brief on Shalhi had been prepared by the GID, Qadhafi's new General Investigation Directorate whose writ covered all problems of state security, external as well as internal. It operated with sophisticated Egyptian advice and technical assistance on the principle that attack was the best form of defence, and had rapidly penetrated the ring of Libyan exiles in Rome, driving the more dangerous among them out of Italy altogether.

The GID suspected that Shalhi was up to something but they did not know what, and the uncertainty was said to be causing a good deal of anxiety in the ranks of Qadhafi's twelve-man Revolutionary Command Council. In mid-summer 1970 the RCC had directed the GID to get him, and a tip-off about this had brought Ubaid, the eternal middleman, on to the scene.

The brief was detailed. It mentioned that Shalhi was well-known at both the Intercontinental and the more luxurious lakeside President Hotel in Geneva, particularly to the well informed Italian barman at the President whom the GID had pinpointed for possible recruitment. Shalhi, it said, was a man who liked to drink and would occasionally let his hair down.

The Libyans knew all about the Geneva house and its staff, about the Maserati and the Mercedes, about the flats in Vienna and London. They had the addresses, the phone numbers, even the purchase prices. They knew which Swiss banks held Shalhi's wealth, who was his personal physician, and the names of women known to him. The GID were looking for points of penetration into his pattern of life, and fancied that a girl would be an excellent one. The brief included the telephone number of a London madam known to procure call-girls for visiting Arabs. Kent was given a list of Shalhi's business associates, among them an Iranian, a German Swiss and an Italian. He was told that years earlier Shalhi had had a close relationship with a German woman who now lived in Berlin . . .

By the end of Kent's twenty-four hour stay at the Cavalieri Hilton, one of the world's best Hiltons, it was agreed that he should personally put a proposal for Shalhi's abduction to Major Abd al-Munaim al-Huni, Libya's intelligence chief. He was to call on the Libyan ambassador in Rome on 15 October to pick up his visa for Tripoli.

Before he could keep this date Kent had to put in some time on Shalhi's own assignment. Reynolds had reported that the principal was getting restive, that he could not quite understand why the British team had been paid off without firing a shot in anger, or why a French team was now preferred. This was the opportunity Kent had been waiting for to make direct contact with the man at the top, and so rid himself of the problems of having Reynolds as intermediary. He suggested to Reynolds that he was better placed to give Shalhi the explanations he wanted. Reynolds jumped at the offer. It would, he thought, be politic—and would keep the money flowing—if the reassuringly professional figure of

Kent were now produced.

Accordingly the two men flew to Geneva on 30
September. Observing what he considered security,
Reynolds insisted that they pretend not to know each
other on the trip and sit in different parts of the
first-class compartment. The meeting with Shalhi was
to take place in the passengers' lounge of the airport
itself, after which Reynolds and Kent were to return
by the next plane to London.

There was no opportunity for long explanations as
Shalhi kept this first meeting to a very quick, almost
clandestine contact. He was not happy to have Kent
sprung on him. When Kent, who had hung back, came
up to the bookstall where Reynolds and Shalhi were
talking, and said, 'I'd very much like a word with
you, Mr Shalhi,' the Arab was taken aback: 'Who told
you my name?' Kent passed the matter off by
suggesting that Shalhi was too well-known a personality to go unrecognised, and was introduced in his
turn as the man who could deliver the 'sharp end'.

Little more was said, but for Kent it was an
important moment, marking his acceptance at the
centre of the action. It had been worth the round trip
from London for the brief exchange by the bookstall.
He now had a direct and personal link with the
principal. He had been given a phone number where
he could reach Shalhi and a rendezvous back in
Geneva a week later. It was becoming evident that in
this operation, with matters too sensitive to be
discussed on open telephone lines, messages would
have to be carried personally from one centre to
another. Someone had to coordinate strategy, someone had to do the rounds of European capitals. It

would, Kent realised, have to be him.

Over the next six weeks Kent was as often in the air as on the ground. In London there were military briefings with the planners. In Rome, where the counterplot was unfolding, Kent had to play his lonely poker game. In Geneva he had to report almost every other day to Shalhi. In Paris the French team was taking shape—and Kent was being pressed for money.

Léon was not at this stage asking for large sums in cash—the front money was relatively modest—so much as for an assurance that his team's wages, 5,000 dollars for each of them, were well and truly in the bank. It is a prerequisite of mercenary operations that such funding is guaranteed in advance. Shalhi recognised this necessity but, naturally enough, did not want to pay until he could see something for his money. He had agreed without demur to Reynolds's original estimate of a global cost of 173,000 dollars, but was growing impatient as the budget showed signs of breaking through this ceiling. The arms and the boat—Reynolds's responsibilities—had swallowed up a sizeable slice, paying off the British had not been cheap administrative expenses were already costing thousands of dollars a week, and he was now being asked for no less than an extra 125,000 for the French team. Relations were a trifle frosty when the three men met again at Geneva on 5 October.

As ever Shalhi's security was good. When Kent and Reynolds collected their Hertz car from Cointrin airport park, Shalhi joined them from his own vehicle, and the conference took place in the anonymous traffic of the autoroute to Lausanne. Kent was at the wheel, while Shalhi and Reynolds argued it out on the back seat. When tempers had cooled and encouraging progress reports been made, Shalhi agreed to give Kent a draft on an American bank in Zurich for 125,000 dollars. Before the car was turned in, it had been decided that the Hilton assignment would be launched four weeks later on 6 November from Bari on the Adriatic coast of Italy. Kent would make sure the team was there, ready to embark on a fast boat provided by Reynolds. On the short voyage to Tripoli the men would be armed and briefed for the task ahead.

Kent was now in a position to reassure Léon. He turned Shalhi's draft into twenty-five bank certified cheques of 5,000 dollars each, made out in the names of the men chosen to go in, and, having shown them to Léon, locked them up in a safe deposit in Geneva. In addition he took out insurance against possible permanent injury or death, but to a large extent the experienced French mercenaries proved they could look after themselves. Each man bought his own three months' cover, and this time Kent judged it unnecessary to plan the operation down to the last hospital bedpan.

One vital element in the operation was under Shalhi's exclusive control. This was intelligence at the Libyan end. It had been necessary to send in Miller and Reynolds for further details of the prison and to select a beach, and now Reynolds was planning a second trip to lay on trucks to carry the invading force from the beach to the Hilton walls—and back again. But information on the political climate in Tripoli, on potential support for a counter-coup, on the detailed provisions for the insurgency which the released prisoners would lead—all these were to be Shalhi's contribution.

Meeting him repeatedly throughout the month of October, Kent was kept abreast of reports brought by courier to Geneva. Léon needed cast-iron assurances that his men were not walking into the arms of a reception committee, and Shalhi had promised that the date of the landing would remain a close secret between himself, Kent and Reynolds. It would never in any circumstances be communicated to anyone on the other side, however loyal, lest he should fall into the hands of Qadhafi's security men. From the Europeans' point of view, a comforting consideration was that Shalhi was going in with the team. In preparation he was taking strenuous exercise and had even acquired a pedometer, on which he dutifully clocked up not less than five miles a day.

At this point Kent learned that the principal was not the only Arab he had to deal with. Shalhi had an associate, a cautious, thorough Libyan merchant who, though in a subordinate position, acted as far as possible as a corrective to Shalhi's impulsiveness. Shalhi was a why-wasn't-it-done-yesterday man, while his partner, on the contrary, seemed reassured by difficulties, as if he did not entirely trust things which went smoothly. For the purposes of the assignment Shalhi was codenamed Bill and his partner William. The names were figleaves, flimsy cover to muddy the trail for an investigator or confuse an eavesdropper.

Unlike Shalhi William was not born to power and wealth, but in a series of business deals in the 1960s had progressed from Volkswagen to Chevrolet and then to Buick and Mercedes—the classic pattern for middle-class Libya in that decade. With Abd al-Aziz al-Shalhi (whom he knew much better than Umar), he had been involved in the BAC air defence deal, and had been visiting the British manufacturers on the eve of the coup. News of Qadhafi's takeover reached him in Rome on his way home, thus saving him from prison. When life as an exile in Rome became dangerous, he announced his departure for the United States, but in fact took out a Chad passport in another name and went to ground in Germany and Switzerland.

Living in hotels, cut off from his wife and family in Tripoli, and not nearly as well-heeled as Shalhi, William was a lonely man. He was bravely going in with the team to do a job which nothing in his life had prepared him for. But like many Arabs he made a hobby of hand-weapons, owning several pistols which he cherished. He would reminisce nostalgically about target practice with Pepsi-Cola bottles on the beaches near Tripoli.

Shalhi used William as a front man to reduce the dangers of too frequent contact between himself and other members of the operation, and it was with William that Kent worked out banking arrangements, and through him that he agreed on expenditure. The currency for the assignment was the dollar, still the most acceptable, the most freely convertible in the world. All purchases, however big or small, were made in cash, but with the dollar depreciating over the weeks, Kent came to wish he was handling yen. Gradually Shalhi grew to have more confidence in Kent and to take him into his counsel. On 25

October, with eleven days to go to D-Day, the two men spent long hours in Geneva going over every detail of the plan.

That day Shalhi gave Kent two letters to be delivered if the counter-coup triumphed but if Shalhi himself were killed in the assault. The first was to King Idris, in which Umar handed back the liberated kingdom to his sovereign and adoptive father. The second was to be James Kent's reward and the bonus for the other participants. It was addressed to Umar's brother Abd al-Aziz and read simply: 'Please pay my friend James Kent the sum of four million dollars for his contribution to our cause.' Originally Kent and Shalhi had agreed on a fee of two million for the successful completion of the assignment, but when it came to writing the figure, Shalhi doubled it. 'The sum is irrelevant,' he said. 'It could be twenty million. It's a negligible amount. We need only divert a part of one day's oil royalties to pay you and recover all our expenses.' Kent added the documents to the cheques in the safe deposit. The four million dollars would be a fortune, but it was still less than the price proposed for handing over Shalhi to the Libyans.

Twenty-four hours later he was in Rome bargaining with a Libyan intelligence captain for the life of his principal. He had called as planned on the Libyan ambassador on 15 October to collect his visa, and was about to fly to Tripoli, coolly aware of the risks he was running, when a message reached him postponing his date with Major al-Huni. Instead a young officer had been sent to settle terms with him in Rome.

Playing for time Kent proposed to undertake a three-month intensive feasibility study costing 60,000 dollars. He said he would have to put Shalhi under surveillance by a four-man team and examine the pattern of his movements to see what opportunities for kidnapping might arise. In any country with a coastline, it would be easy to seize him, take him by car to the beach, put him in a small boat and hand him over to the Libyans at sea. But in landlocked Switzerland, where he was well guarded, there were many problems. Kent outlined these at length to make himself credible. If it was so bloody easy why did they not do it themselves? If they did not like his terms, they could try someone else.

'And after the study, you will do it?' the Libyan officer asked. Kent explained that it was no use undertaking a feasibility study if you promised to do the job anyway. The captain seemed not to grasp this point and the argument showed signs of going on endlessly. He was an idealistic young man, convinced of the righteousness of locking Shalhi up though appalled that it would cost the revolution two million pounds to have it done. As the young Libyan flew home, Kent reflected that before Qadhafi and his RCC could agree the price, they might well be dead or in exile themselves. All he needed was ten days' grace and Shalhi would be speeding to Tripoli with his mercenaries.

While all this high-level financial negotiating was taking place in Geneva and Rome, the nuts and bolts of the Hilton assignment were being put together in different places around Europe. In Paris Léon had his team ready to entrain for Bari. In Brussels Thompson was assembling step-ladders, webbing equipment and other bits of minor gear. The arms

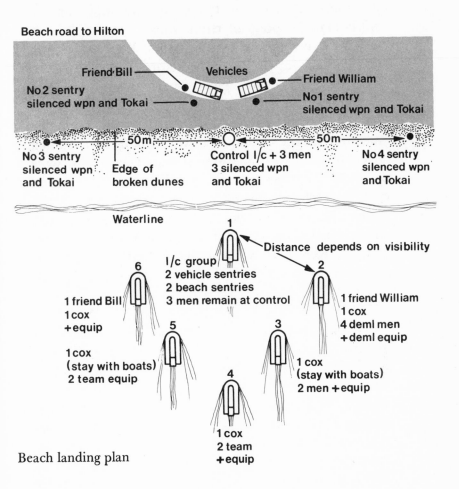

Beach road to Hilton

Friend Bill — Vehicles — Friend William

No 2 sentry
silenced wpn and Tokai

No 1 sentry
silenced wpn and Tokai

No 3 sentry
silenced wpn
and Tokai

Edge of
broken dunes

50m

Control I/c + 3 men
3 silenced wpn
and Tokai

50m

No 4 sentry
silenced wpn
and Tokai

Waterline

1

I/c group
2 vehicle sentries
2 beach sentries
3 men remain at control

Distance depends on visibility

6

1 friend Bill
1 cox
+ equip

2

1 friend William
1 cox
4 deml men
+ deml equip

5

1 cox
(stay with boats)
2 team equip

3

1 cox
(stay with boats)
2 men + equip

4

1 cox
2 team
+ equip

Beach landing plan

and explosives were being made ready to go by air from Prague to Dubrovnik on the Dalmatian coast. Reynolds's ship was no doubt already sailing up the Adriatic to the point of rendezvous.

On the last day of October 1970 Kent saw Shalhi and William for the last time before they were due to meet on the beach near Bari, ready for action. Everything was dove-tailing smoothly, El Dorado was in sight, and the pent up excitement of the three men meeting in the room in downtown Geneva spilled over into rather macabre jokes. The Arabs were planning to travel light to Tripoli: either they would collect a change of shirt from their homes on the other side, or they would not be needing shirts any more. It was a moment of tension and euphoria. 'Christ,' Kent said, 'we're going to do it!'

8 Appointment at Bari

Five hectic days before blast-off James Kent was landed with a problem, the sort of petty administrative chore which eats time and corrodes the nerves. At this late hour Léon had been forced to make some changes in his team of ex-legionnaires and parachutists, and the carefully prepared pay-cheques in the safe deposit at Geneva would have to be altered. One man's passport had expired, and could not be renewed in time, so he had to be dropped. A couple of others had from long habit given false names and now were worried that without official papers to match they might have trouble turning Kent's drafts into dollars. The pay-off is understandably much on a mercenary's mind. It is what he bickers about most. For a horrible moment on 1 November it looked as if Léon had a small mutiny on his hands, so the next morning Kent had to take the Paris plane to Geneva, retrieve the cheques, take them to the bank in Zurich which had issued them, make the suitable emendations, photocopy the lot for the team in France, and return the precious packet to the safe deposit. It took the best part of a day. By the evening Léon's strike force was back in the front line.

While Kent was shuttling round Europe that
Monday, Sir Alec Douglas-Home, the British Foreign
Secretary in the new Tory government, was enter-
taining in London Libya's deputy prime minister
Major Abd al-Salam Jallud. The Libyan had come to
wind up the massive BAC air defence deal which Abd
al-Aziz al-Shalhi had secured for King Idris. There was
some sticky bargaining to be done: a matter of £32
million which the old regime had paid on account and
Qadhafi now wanted to recover, but which the British
Aircraft Corporation claimed he had forfeited by
cancelling the contract. Jallud argued that the British
government had pressured Idris into buying this
expensive military toy and must therefore assume
responsibility for the debt. In the pistol-at-your-head
manner of Qadhafi's diplomacy, Jallud backed up his
argument with the threat of pulling Libyan money
out of London. Not surprisingly Sir Alec had been
anxious to prevent his fellow Scottish grandee David
Stirling from rocking this delicate boat.

At twenty-seven the quick, crafty Jallud was the
second most powerful man in Libya. Short, dark,
with a long-nosed Italian face, this obscure, untrained
young man had burst upon the international scene as
a first-class negotiator and manager of Libya's multi-
million dollar economy. In a few brief months he had
successfully talked the British and Americans out of
their bases in Libya, riled the British and wooed the
French by spending a hundred million dollars on
Mirage aircraft, and bludgeoned the oil companies
operating in Libya into paying the host government
an extra thirty cents a barrel, so boosting Qadhafi's
oil revenues to 1,500 million dollars a year.

But in London in November 1970 Jallud did not make much headway. He was intensely suspicious of the British—they had, after all, been the main power behind Idris's throne—and his sentiments were fully reciprocated in Whitehall. What he did not know, and would not have believed had he been told, was that the Foreign Office had done its damnedest to throttle the Hilton assignment at birth.

Annette, Léon's twenty-three-year-old mistress, was part-owner of a small working-men's café which her French father and Indo-Chinese mother ran in a backstreet off the Avenue Victor Hugo in Paris. A favourite haunt for mercenaries, the bar, with its half-dozen tables and its one telephone on the wall, served as Léon's recruiting office, communications centre and operational headquarters.

The men who drifted to the café were a different breed from Watchguard's ex-SAS types. While the British had been tough, resourceful, disciplined, the French were cold, killer-hard, experienced—a good deal more suitable, James Kent reflected, for this ruthless in-and-out operation in which it was more than likely that any stray Libyan surprising the landing party would have to be knifed. He liked dealing with the French, who were adventurers but not criminals, an important distinction. Like criminals, mercenaries take risks for gain, but whereas the criminal is a flawed personality, the mercenary must be able to act under a collective discipline alien to the criminal. What is more, a mercenary by definition is involved in a political act: if he turns his specialist skills and nerves to robbing banks, he ceases to be a mercenary.

Léon had the knack of finding not just men, but the right men, the sort of quick-thinking operators who might be prepared to hijack the entire gold reserves of a black African country but would never dream of taking a franc from an old lady in the street. To an incredible degree they were stock characters, confirming the popular myth that French mercenaries were the product of the divided loyalties and shady political intrigue of colonial wars. Many had links with Algeria, most had seen service in the mercenary wars of the 1960s. Apart from the French in Léon's team, there was a German ex-legionnaire, a Belgian, and bizarrely a former British Grenadier Guardsman of dual Anglo-French nationality who could be useful as an interpreter.

The team knew they were in for a rough-house, but no more than Léon did they have any clear idea of where they were being sent or whom they would be fighting. All they were told was that this was a cross-border, arms-running foray in which they could expect resistance from the forces of the government concerned.

The task facing Léon and his number two, Jules, was to deliver this motley crew to pre-arranged small hotels in Bari by the night of Thursday, 5 November, in the least conspicuous manner. For reasons of security, not expense, they were to go by train rather than on the daily flight to Bari. Tickets for the journey were bought in twos and threes at different times and the men despatched on different trains from the Gare de Lyon. With plenty of trains on the first lap to Rome, there was no problem in staggering departures, but between Rome and Bari the possibilities were more limited, and men so obviously foreign travelling in larger batches could only hope not to be observed. There was one casualty. A member of the team turned up at the station in Paris with his girl-friend, and was axed.

Jules travelled with the advance party of the team while Léon and Jean-Louis, the interpreter, joined Jeff Thompson in Brussels. This trio packed Jeff's compromising gear into a hired van and made it by road to Bari in a fast thirty hours' travelling. Jeff, blunt British Warrant officer that he was, spoke not a word of French, hated French food and shared the English mercenaries' traditional contempt for their French counterparts as an inefficient and disorderly crowd. But amazingly enough he got on well with Léon and developed a sneaking regard for his men.

James Kent made the journey alone and by air from Paris to Rome, only to find when about to board his connection for Bari that the airline had mislaid his luggage. It was a clammy November day, hardly the weather to find oneself without a change of clothes. Kent was not a man to let himself be bullied by airport officialdom, and had the place turned upside down (without success), almost missing the late night plane in the process. By such trifles is the fate of nations decided.

Bari had been chosen as the port of embarkation only after many other places had been considered and rejected. It was thought undesirable to use a French port from which to mount the operation as, together with the use of a French team, this might be stretching French official tolerance to breaking point.

Greece had advantages—the right sort of little islands, well spread out, where a boat could anchor unobtrusively to take the team on. But almost as soon as the possibility was raised, the planners turned it down, fearing a showdown with the watchful Greek colonels who might construe the Libyan job as a plot against themselves. Spain seemed equally inhospitable, and the thought of doing lengthy time in a Spanish jail was unattractive. So Bari it was. Compared to the police regimes of Greece and Spain, the Italians seemed agreeably feckless, and there was always the hope that, smarting from the expulsion of Italians from Libya, the authorities might in an emergency lend a hand or at least look the other way.

James Kent was the first to arrive. On the night of Wednesday, 4 November, he booked into the second best hotel in Bari, a rather depressed establishment well below the standards he was accustomed to. There was a crack in the bath, only one towel, and the telephone service depended on the caprice of an aggravatingly unhurried reception clerk. Barely had he arrived when this clerk passed him an incoming call from London. Miller was on the line to say that Steve Reynolds's ship's agent, a man called Claude Perrault whom Kent was due to meet the next day, was clamouring for an extra three thousand dollars to cover urgent repairs. Unless the money was paid immediately, the boat might be late at the rendezvous.

This message sent Kent speeding to the post office to cable Zurich for a transfer. Swiss banks are efficient; at noon the next day, he walked out of the local branch of the Banca di Napoli a millionaire in lire. By then Jeff and Léon were sleeping off their non-stop drive in a *pensione* and the rest of the team was trickling into the town after an arduous thirty-six hours in the train. Bill and William—the Arab principals had rather ostentatiously adopted their code-names for the trip—were for security reasons staying in Brindisi, one hundred kilometres south of Bari, until the last moment. They were driving up to Bari that Thursday evening and would be waiting with their light luggage, ready to be picked up from the lounge of the Hôtel Mediterranée.

It was judged unwise for the ship with its cargo of arms to put in at Bari harbour. Instead it would drop anchor a few hundred yards off a beach fifteen kilometres south of the town, and which could be readily identified at night by the lighthouse at Monopoli nearby. The boat was expected at 11 p.m. Léon's men would board it after midnight, followed an hour later by Bill and William, and the ship would sail before dawn, leaving Kent and Jeff to keep a lonely vigil for the team's return.

A man had been despatched to lie up in the dunes above the beach and signal the boat to its moorings. Late in the afternoon Kent drove out to see that all was well. It was a perfect spot, away from all habitation. The sea was flat and calm under a low sky. Below him the coast formed a sheltered cove where a Zodiac landingcraft from the ship could put in for the men.

Not a hitch, not a compromising hoofmark anywhere. The men, the guns and the boat should be nearing their preordained meeting place, and no authority in the world could object. The expedition would be exposed only when it entered Libyan territorial waters. No hostile posture would be struck until it was practically on target.

A drizzling rain set in. Claude Perrault was an appalling twenty minutes late for his six o'clock appointment with Kent on the deserted road above the beach, a delay in this meticulous scenario which had the professional intelligence man's blood boiling. Worse still, when Perrault at last drove up to claim his money it was with the news that engine trouble had put back the ship's arrival from Yugoslavia by a few hours. He was horribly vague about where the ship had broken down and seemed not even to know which port it was now at. Was it at Split or Rijeka or had it crossed to an Italian harbour?

Kent knew he could freeze the situation for no more than twenty-four hours. Léon's men were keyed up for action, and their morale, not to mention their security, would go to pieces if they were kept inexplicably hanging about. The principals would have to return to their Brindisi hotel.

Kent raced back to Bari to call off the count-down. As Thursday night wore on he wrestled with the tiresome Italian telephone service in an attempt to get from London some explanation for the mystery of the boat. But Reynolds had flown that day to Tripoli, allegedly to collect the trucks and drivers and bring them to meet the landing party. He had volunteered to stay on in Libya as a tourist or businessman after the raid—a dangerous assignment in view of all he knew about the operation. At such a distance his control over the movement of the ship was clearly far from perfect.

Friday brought its own bad news. When Perrault arrived that morning, still uncertain of the whereabouts of his boat but offering, if the money was right, to charter another, Kent blew his top. He knew that a new craft could not be conjured up out of thin air in any of the time scales that suited the arms and the men. It was crazy to suppose that twenty-five desperate characters could be kept out of trouble in the south of Italy while Perrault produced a boat from somewhere in northern Europe. The hideous thought struck him that perhaps there had never been a boat, and that Perrault was taking them all for a colossal ride.

No boat but also, it now appeared, no arms. London came on the line in the afternoon with the chilling information that the Yugoslav authorities had impounded the entire consignment of hardware at Dubrovnik and had arrested the agent with them into the bargain.

Kent could scarcely credit it. The whole shooting match had come adrift. That bloody amateur Reynolds, with his big talk and bigger spending, had let them down. But totally. Kent raged against the absent Reynolds who had left him the grim job of breaking the news to the principals, now back in the Hôtel Méditerranée, waiting with their oilskins and plimsolls to be taken to the beach.

It was a grisly moment. Being the bearer of bad tidings is not pleasant, especially when one feels that failure could have been avoided. Would his credibility stand up? The Arabs had met no one except Reynolds and himself. They might suspect that the team, the boat, the arms and everything else he had told them were pure invention.

In this sticky situation, Kent decided that his first move should be to introduce Jeff Thompson to the principals. Jeff had been witness to the weeks of effort and planning, to the frustrations and difficulties they had overcome on their way to Bari. His quiet, laconic manner might help win the Arabs' confidence. Jeff embarked on a technical account of the explosives needed to breach the Hilton's walls. It worked.

Leaving Jeff talking to William, Kent took Shalhi aside and played his ace. He told him the full story of the counterplot—about the meetings in Paris and Rome, the detailed brief prepared by Qadhafi's police, the Libyan businessman who hoped the abduction would make his fortune. 'How much did you say Qadhafi would pay for me? Two million pounds?' Shalhi was delighted with this tribute to his importance. He had heard from other sources that the Libyans had put out a contract for him to an assassination squad, and was heartened to learn that the contract had come to Kent. After this bonus the news that the Hilton assignment had collapsed was easier to swallow.

For the second time a mercenary team had to be paid off. They had not earned their full five thousand dollars but they got enough to keep them happy. The next day Léon shepherded his men on to trains to Paris. Kent flew to Rome, arriving just in time to see the plane carrying his mislaid suitcase take off for Bari. It was the last straw. In his soiled suit he settled down in the airport lounge for the long wait while the telex got busy to bring the suitcase back on the next plane.

There was rage in his heart. He had put himself at risk in an operation he did not fully control. All the work and effort had been wasted, and though he had not been responsible for the fiasco he was very conscious that some of the blame must rub off on him. On Sunday, 8 November 1970, James Kent flew to Geneva and made his way to the downtown meeting place for very serious discussions with his principal.

9 The Inquisitor

Back to square one. Upwards of 200,000 dollars spent and nothing to show for it except a lot of loose ends strewn across Europe from Brussels to Bari. A shaming legacy of blunders. It was a cold, gusty evening when James Kent flew into Geneva for his scheduled meeting with Shalhi on Sunday, 8 November 1970. The Hilton assignment was at its lowest ebb.

In a secret operation, failure breeds recrimination and guilt, but above all suspicion. After the fiasco of the impounded arms and the phantom boat, Kent for his part could afford to trust no one—with the sole exception of Shalhi himself. But was he trusted in return? There were two items in his personal ledger which Shalhi has a right to wonder about: his involvement in the counterplot, which could be interpreted in more than one way—not all of them reassuring; and his former official background, which the Arab now knew about. The British had intervened against Shalhi once, and he had every reason to ask himself whether Kent had not been planted on him to guarantee failure. He had to face the various possibilities that Kent was there for the Libyans, or for the British, or simply for the money, to lay his hands on as large a sum as possible and then disappear.

But then Shalhi remembered Kent's genuine fury at Bari. The Englishman had shown qualities of dogged determination and precise planning. He invariably kept his appointments and his promises. Of all the components of the operation, his alone—the mercenary team—had been delivered to Bari on time. The greater the frustrations, the more resolved he appeared to overcome them, as if his reputation as a professional were at stake. It was almost an emotional commitment. Even more heartening for Shalhi was Kent's ideological position in the affair, disapproving of Qadhafi and clearly supporting Shalhi's right to try and regain what King Idris and he had lost. Of course Kent liked to live well, of course money was important to him, but his motives were by no means only material. He was hooked by the job.

In spite of the setback at Bari, in spite of the hole in his funds, Shalhi was unequivocally determined to carry on. His analysis of the problem had not changed. He needed a foreign mercenary force as much as ever, and Kent, who had been in it from the beginning and who knew so much, had become indispensable.

As a result the post mortem at Geneva was less fraught than Kent had anticipated. Shalhi brought William to the meeting, and to the two Arabs Kent outlined the three essential questions they had to answer:

Did they still have a team? Léon's men looked

good at Bari, but the morale of a mercenary is a
fragile thing. Without the stiffening of military
discipline, he is ultra-sensitive to the possibility of
disaster, and the slightest hitch in an operation of this
kind has him running for cover. Could Léon rally his
team a second time?

Could the arms—fifty-five crates held by the police
at Dubrovnik—be retrieved? If they were lost, was
there money to repeat the order?

Could they afford to buy a boat? Kent's experience since the fruitless Malta trip had convinced him
that a boat would have to be bought, not hired. They
would need total control over its movements and its
crew. Did they have that sort of money?

Kent had a fourth point to make. If the principals
wanted him in on the Hilton assignment, they could
have him on the condition that he was appointed
chief executive, master of the planning, the budget
and the men. He had to be inquisitor as well as
co-ordinator, getting to the bottom of what had gone
wrong before rebuilding the assignment, brick by
brick, on unshakeable foundations. He was asking
them not only for a massive new financial commitment, but for authority to speak and act on their
behalf.

So James Kent set the lethal machine rolling again.
He had agreed with Shalhi and William that, with all
the work to be done and the threat of seasonal storms
in the Mediterranean, the assault should be delayed
until a suitable date in February. But that winter was
not to be a joy-ride. The gaiety and excitement of the
first stage had gone, leaving a long, cold grind. It was
not a mild winter, 1970-1971, but one sharpened

with an icy blast which seemed to come from the Siberian steppe. Flying in poor conditions, he was frequently diverted from one fog-bound airport to another scarcely more hospitable. And then there were the bomb and hijacking scares, the constant aggravating searches of his luggage and himself, the havoc played with timetables. In spite of the satisfactions of his numbered duck at the Tour d'Argent in Paris, in spite of the appreciative deference of the head waiter in the Red Room at Sacher's in Vienna, in spite of an orgy of antepasta chez Valentino at Geneva, Kent was not enjoying it any more.

At the back of his mind was the constant awareness that somewhere in the interlocking complexities of plot and counterplot there might have been a leak, some overlooked clue which might betray his double role to the Libyans. If they discovered what he was up to, they would not be tender. There are many ways a man can have an accident, from a loosened car wheel or a blow on the head to the loss of his passport. So Kent was circumspect, his departures and arrivals sudden and unannounced. No one could lay an ambush for him. To hotel servants he seemed a prosperous businessman, for ever flying between board meetings, very clear about what he wanted, but wanting it fast, always in a hurry, always on the telephone. Meals were the only leisure he allowed himself.

His first task was to sort out the goodies from the baddies, to identify whom he could trust. Suspicion is the disease of the secret agent, inevitably more acute when things go wrong. This time Kent decided he should not take David Stirling into confidence

because Stirling's loyalties were to the British: if
Stirling felt the assignment conflicted with his own
strong views or with official policy, he might talk to
the authorities. John Brooke Miller was a problem
because he would talk to Stirling, but he could still be
valuable as a military adviser. The stalwart Jeff
Thompson was beyond question a good guy. So was
Léon. William? The thought crossed Kent's mind
that William might have reinsured with the other side.
His positive pleasure in difficulties was almost
worrying, raising the possibility that he was being
paid to slow things down. And yet this lonely man
had sacrificed so much that Kent had not the heart to
think ill of him.

Steve Reynolds was more of a problem. Kent had
no grounds for believing the South African a traitor
or a con man, but his romantic attitude towards
secret operations, his amateur incompetence had
from the beginning spelled nothing but trouble. But
Reynolds knew too much and had been too central to
the action to be dropped. In the interests of security
he would have to be kept on board, given his share of
the reward, but phased slowly out of the action without knowing it.

There was a tense scene in London when Kent had
to break the news to Reynolds that he was now in
charge. 'I'm sorry, you've had your chance,' he said.
'It has to be played this way, or the principals will
call the whole thing off.' Reynolds blustered for a
while, then accepted the new situation, but the slight
was to rankle.

Kent's next call was Paris to see Léon who invited
him out to dinner at a restaurant in Les Halles. Léon

arrived with Annette in a new car, acquired to console her for a miscarriage. As usual he had paid only the deposit. If it was possible to pay by instalments, he never bought anything cash down on the sensible argument that he might not live to complete the payments. Given the perilous life Léon chose to lead, such proofs of prudent calculation were as refreshing as they were unexpected.

Léon reported that his men were none the worse for their *rendezvous manqué* and could be assembled again at short notice. He offered to put a little unsubtle pressure on Claude Perrault at Geneva to retrieve the money spent on the boat that never turned up. If anyone needed sorting out Léon and a couple of friends could do it. But Kent decided that at this stage security was more important than vindictiveness.

Two members of the French team came from Marseilles and were seamen of a kind. Could they, Kent asked, look out for a suitable boat, large enough to carry the men and the bulky cargo of arms, and fast enough for a hit-and-run job? Léon promised to set his men to work immediately, and ten days later, on 19 November, summoned Kent back to Paris with the news that a possible vessel had been located in a Toulon boatyard. It was one of two coastal patrol boats whose present owner was prepared, if the money was right, to cannibalise one craft in order to make the other seaworthy. The purchase price was 50,000 dollars, on top of which between thirty and forty thousand would be needed for the refit.

With Shalhi's agreement to the figures, Kent flew south on the 22nd to interview a four-man crew and check the boat. Built in Bremen in 1957, powered by twin Mercedes six-cylinder engines generating about 750 horsepower, Conquistador XIII could do about eighteen knots. She was fast enough for their purposes; but was she big enough? Normally she would carry no more than a dozen men. The full team and crew could, at a pinch, be packed on board, but if they were challenged such numbers would take some explaining away. In summer they could pretend to be deep-sea diving or otherwise disporting themselves, but in winter so large a body of men on so small a craft could look sinister.

The crew consisted of a captain, a first officer, an engineer and a deckhand who was expected to help out in the galley. All four were contacts of the mariners in Léon's team, brought in on the understanding that they were to take part in a smuggling run. Kent liked the blond bearded first officer, but the captain did not seem the right calibre for a secret expedition. He knew the Mediterranean and had a boat of his own, but he was a moaner, raising difficulties and demanding payment when none was due.

In spite of these misgivings Kent decided that the boat and crew would have to do, and after a trip to Zurich to collect 50,000 dollars in 100-dollar bills, he was back in the South of France, eating a solitary lunch in the only restaurant open on the rain-swept harbour at St Tropez, before driving on to Toulon to take possession of the boat.

Then there was the problem of registration. Conquistador needed a flag, but for this job she could not afford to be bound by the normal regulations and standards of maritime powers, involving crew, cargo and function. So it had to be a flag of convenience, such as provided by Panama and Liberia. As it happened, Liberia was just then tightening up its rules of registration following a tanker collision in the English Channel, and Kent was left with only one option. Through agents in Panama City he acquired a readymade company for 750 dollars to take ownership of the vessel. Then he sent Jeff Thompson to complete the registration with the Panamanian consulate general at Genoa.

For reasons of security Kent judged it vital to keep his organisation small, and this meant a certain doubling of roles, as in an understaffed *Hamlet* in which Polonius turns up later as the gravedigger. But a good gravedigger does not always make a good Polonius. Jeff, the thoroughly English sharp-end soldier, was given the task of representing Kent in the Toulon boatyard, controlling the purse-strings there, dickering with the French workmen and crew and generally equipping Conquistador for the sea. He was to spend most of six weeks on the Riviera, making sure that by mid-January 1971 the boat was fully ready to sail round the toe of Italy and into the action zone. Admirable as a fighting man, he was an uneasy administrator, and the strain affected his nerves.

In contrast with the smooth and rapid progress made in launching Conquistador XIII, the arms saga proved murky, expensive and labyrinthine. As any dealer will admit, credit in the arms trade is unheard of, trust does not exist, and double-crossing is a routine hazard.

When the Hilton assignment came to pieces at Bari, all that James Kent could learn was that for reasons unknown the Yugoslav authorities were holding not only the arms and explosives but the passport of the agent in charge of them. Tens of thousands of dollars were tied up in those crates. Kent resolved to find out the facts, identify the men responsible for the failure, and, if possible, retrieve the weapons. In the event it took him a month of confrontations with Reynolds, of enduring evasions, demands for more money, inconclusive meetings and broken promises before he began to trace the outlines of the story.

The trail led from Reynolds to an obscure baronet (whom Reynolds had co-opted to help, believing perhaps that a title might add respectability), and from him to a Central European contact man, Gregor Jirasek. The baronet agreed to arrange for Kent to meet Gregor in the Metropole Hotel, Belgrade, at 7 p.m. on Sunday, 6 December 1970.

As a precaution Kent booked in at two hotels, the Metropole in the centre of Belgrade and the newer Yugoslavia overlooking the Danube: he slept in one and made his phone calls from the other. Seven o'clock came and went without Gregor appearing. Kent waited, feeling very depressed, lonely and bad-tempered, and apparently wasting his time. Still no Gregor. Coldly furious he telephoned Reynolds, then the baronet in London for an explanation, and was met with more evasions to which, his temper breaking, he responded with a stream of abuse. The baronet kept saying 'I can't hear you.' He could. Kent repeated his insults and the receiver was slammed down in London, but not before Kent had learned

Gregor's telephone number in Vienna.

He put through a call to Austria, and at last made contact with the man who knew the facts. A courteous, strongly accented voice answered him: 'Ah, Mr Kent, how kind of you to telephone! No, I had no arrangement to meet you, but you are very fortunate. I have here in my office Mr Higgins who has been looking after this affair.' It was the first time Kent had heard of any Mr Higgins, but he was relieved to be getting somewhere at last and did not press for clarification. It was agreed that the mysterious Higgins and Gregor would meet him at Vienna airport at twelve noon in two days' time off the flight from Munich.

Before leaving Belgrade he called on a Yugoslav lawyer to ask him to find out by what authority the arms were held. Spurred on by an advance paid in dollars, the lawyer took very little time to discover that the whole matter had been passed to the jurisdiction of the army in the Zagreb military district, and that no civilian string-pulling was possible. Confronted with the impenetrability of the Yugoslav military machine, and with nothing to go on but a vague promise from Vienna, Kent was driven to the conclusion that the consignment of arms was almost certainly irretrievable—at least within the tight schedule of the assignment. If he got them back in time, it would be a welcome bonus, but meanwhile a second lot would have to be bought.

An odd trio was waiting for him at the barrier at Vienna airport on Tuesday—a big, bluff, genial Englishman with greying hair, who introduced himself as Frank Higgins and did most of the talking;

his tall, sallow companion whose central European origin was stamped on his face and manners; and a slim woman in her early twenties who never opened her lips. Introduced as Louise, she was, it appeared, Higgins's mistress. She was hung about with chunky gold jewellery which looked as if it came from the tax-free shop at Zurich airport.

Over a long lunch in the airport restaurant, Kent heard an interesting story. Higgins, it emerged, was an entrepreneur on the fringes of the arms business, living a house of cards existence from one mercenary war to the next. He had been involved in the sale of aircraft to Biafra, transactions sufficiently informal to make him reluctant to go home to England for the time being. In August a contact of his from the Nigerian conflict had telephoned with a proposition: someone he knew—it turned out to be Reynolds—wanted to buy a small consignment of arms from Czechoslovakia and needed an intermediary to handle the deal on his behalf. Higgins took up the offer and with two Middle European associates, Gregor Jirasek and Stefan Vlček, formed a company for the purpose. Reynolds then sent a shopping list of arms and explosives, together with a twenty per cent down payment, and Higgins, Gregor and Stefan placed the order with Omnipol, the Czechoslovak arms sales agency. On 1 November Reynolds sent an assistant to Prague with forty-five thousand dollars in cash for Gregor—the balance, including commissions and expenses, due on the arms. She handed over the money and returned on the same plane.

Gregor then settled the bill with Omnipol, and

arranged for the consignment to be flown on 5 November from Prague to a Yugoslav airport some fifteen kilometres from the Croatian port of Dubrovnik. He was there himself with trucks to meet the special ČSA freight plane and ferry the fifty-five crates of weapons safely to a customs warehouse in the port where Reynolds's boat was to collect them that same evening.

Gregor then took up the story. He seemed a cultivated man, with a melancholy, rather old-fashioned charm, and a good command of English. The trouble was, he said, the boat never came. After twenty-four hours the port authorities began to be curious about him and his cargo. The customs officers took a more careful look at the documents and way-bills. To their horror they discovered that the consignment contained explosives which should never have come to Dubrovnik in the first place. Under the strict Yugoslav regulations, explosives could be handled only through the little port of Ploče further up the coast. Worse still, the documents accompanying the cases did not include a Yugoslav arms permit, which Reynolds was supposed to have arranged. The cargo was stranded there illegally, and with it Gregor.

The port authorities called in the police, then the military, 'and, Mr Kent, the questioning I was subjected to was highly unpleasant!' What worried the Yugoslavs was that part of the cargo might have been 'lost' between the airport and Dubrovnik, and fallen into the hands of dissident Croatian nationalists. It took Gregor nineteen days of negotiations to prove his innocence, recover his passport and get out of the country.

Gregor was not a professional arms dealer, and
showed signs of grievance at having been dropped in
such a mess. At Higgins's instigation, he pressed into
Kent's hand a detailed note of his expenses and loss
of income for the best part of a month, with dinars
suitably translated into dollars. If only the boat had
arrived on time, he complained, the other mistakes
would not have counted.

The man was patently honest. Kent decided that,
to get things moving, he would settle Gregor's
expenses on the spot and place an immediate repeat
order with Higgins's company. Shalhi had already
paid heavily for them to learn the job, and might as
well profit from their experience. Kent promised
them a twenty per cent down-payment in Geneva the
following day, after which they would together call
on Omnipol in Prague.

In Switzerland he collected through William fifteen
thousand dollars from the float, as usual in 100-dollar
bills, and booked into one of the small suites on the
third floor of the President Hotel overlooking Lake
Geneva. Higgins and Louise put up at the
Intercontinental, and it was there on 11 November
that Kent counted out his dollars on the bedroom
table. He was halfway down the corridor when he
realised that he had left his topcoat behind: he
returned, knocked perfunctorily on the door and
went in. Higgins and Louise had thrown the dollars in
the air and were dancing round the room. It was not a
reassuring sight. Kent picked up his coat and left, a
very troubled man.

He had given his pledge to Shalhi that this time

everything was going to work. The security conscious principals had to remain safely on the fringe of the action, at least until embarkation, and there was no one to tie up the loose ends except Kent, and unless he did it himself, he would not believe it was happening. By this time he felt he had shuffled off some of Reynolds's legacy of failure, but his inquisition was taking its toll. Bari, Belgrade, Vienna, Geneva, the blunders over boat and weapons—all these he had felt with his nerves as well as understood with his intelligence. Now it was to be Prague in the dead of winter.

To go behind the Iron Curtain is for a man of Kent's background always a psychological jump. Western Europe is totally familiar but the East is potentially hostile territory, uncharted and threatening. Anyone with a past in British or American government service is warned about the dangers involved in visiting the Communist bloc: there is always a fear that a security service on the other side might loosen tongues, perhaps with the help of sodium pentathol. Such melodrama apart, it is difficult enough for a Westerner to clear the daily hurdles of life in a people's republic.

When Kent reached Prague on Tuesday, 15 December, Gregor was hovering anxiously at the airport barrier with a downcast face and the sobering news that there was not an hotel room to be had in the city. Kent had cabled from London to reserve a room, but running true to Communist form, Czechoslovakia's scant accommodation was packed to its limits with fraternal delegations from such centres as Havana and Ulan Bator. At the Yalta Hotel, Kent

tried a Western technique. He produced some dollar
bills. The clerk could not push them back across the
counter fast enough, but an hour later he had squared
his Communist conscience and Kent had a room.

A small snag was that Higgins, the man with the
money for the down-payment on the arms, had failed
to turn up. On the international telephone Kent and
Gregor tracked him down to the Parisian comfort of
the Hotel Prince de Galles, where Louise answered
their call with the unconvincing explanation that
Higgins was ill. A moment later Higgins himself came
on the line with a quite different story, but Kent, at
the end of his patience, interrupted with a sinister 'If
you don't telex the money to the account of
Omnipol in Prague immediately I shall have you
sorted out.' Another faulty link in his arrangements
had snapped.

At this awkward moment Gregor produced his
associate Stefan Vlček, a burly, cheerful man with a
tremendous capacity for social contacts. Gregor was
the tall suave Slav with a university education, Stefan
the amiable extrovert who could get things done, the
sort of kindly fixer who remembered whose mother
was ill and brought flowers for her. These two formed
a useful partnership. Kent found them civilised,
sensible—and reassuringly scrupulous. Even had he
been buying safety pins in Czechoslovakia, he would
have needed an agent. In an arms deal Gregor and
Stefan were worth their weight in gold. They seemed
to know their way about the Communist party
hierarchy, and Stefan had first-class contacts at
several levels of Omnipol as well, where Kent needed
them. Things were beginning to look up.

To Kent's relief, the money from Higgins reached Prague within a few hours—minus, however, not only Higgins's own commission but also that of Gregor and Stefan. He made it up to them. From now on, he told them, he wanted to hear no more of Higgins. He would deal with their company and with them.

With these intermediaries, negotiations with Omnipol were painless. Contact had been made at the right levels, and the head of the ·department concerned accepted Kent's invitation to dinner. Gregor had advised Kent that this was how to do business with Omnipol. More could be achieved over a meal than in their offices.

Because of Czechoslovakia's shortage of foreign exchange, Omnipol has contrived to carve out a remarkable independence for itself, selling arms to all buyers—so long as the currency is right: the one currency it will not accept is its own. In return it provides excellent service. Weapons well packed and in first-class condition, are always delivered with a complement of spares and such extras as sling, cleaning kit, bayonet and spare magazine. Instruction manuals in the required language are included. As for the destination, the Czechs require an acceptable end user, stipulating only that the weapons they sell shall not go to Rhodesia, Portugal, South Africa or Israel. Even this can be a formality. Once out of their hands, and providing the size of the order or the weapons themselves are not too large, a consignment can be diverted anywhere in the world without much difficulty. The Czechs prefer not to know.

To comply with the regulations an end user certificate was arranged, made out to a dealer in

Chad. The arms and explosives were to reach Fort
Lamy ostensibly by air to Yugoslavia, then by sea to
the Cameroon port of Douala on the West African
coast, then overland across the Chad frontier. It was
not an unusual route, for to send the consignment all
the way by air would be expensive.

The shopping list catered for two requirements. It
had to equip the strike force and, in a second stage,
the released prisoners. All in all it was a sizeable
arsenal. The basic weapon was the 9 mm submachine
gun, of which 195 were ordered with 40,000 rounds
of ammunition. In additon there were thirty 7.65 mm
automatic rifles (ten with night sights for snipers),
with 30,000 rounds of ammunition, and sixty 7.65
mm machine pistols with 6,000 rounds. In case of
real opposition, the military planners had asked for
four medium machine guns and a dozen anti-tank
rocket launchers, complete with 72 shells. There were
50 high-explosive hand grenades, 100 incendiary
grenades and 60 pressure-operated anti-personnel
mines, equipped with fuses and primers. The list
included silencers for the pistols, shell carriers for the
rocket launchers, extra magazines and machine gun
belts, and four signals pistols.

A separate order for explosives included 75
kilograms of plastic, 1,000 metres of blasting fuse,
1,000 electric detonators, 100 metres of safety fuse
and three blasting machines. The Czechs were able to
supply everything except tear-gas grenades and bipods
for the automatic rifles: Kent decided to do without
these refinements. The rest was all in stock in
different parts of the country and had merely to be
assembled and crated at the right moment. Omnipol

would need seven days' notice and would then send the consignment to the selected destination.

But which destination was it to be? Shalhi had justifiably developed a certain antipathy to Yugoslavia. 'If your hand has been bitten once,' he observed, 'you don't put it back in the same mouth.' Czechoslovakia being land-locked, there was no avoiding moving the arms by air, road, rail or water over or across one or other of her neighbours. Kent asked Gregor if the consignment could be sent north to the Polish port of Gdynia on the Baltic, where he had been told the Czechs had free zone facilities. Kent liked the idea because it took things right away from the Mediterranean, fitted reasonably well with the Chad cover story and would give the men a better chance, on the Atlantic haul round Spain, to test the weapons at sea without fear of detection. They could then pass quickly through the Straits of Gibraltar in fighting form.

But the Polish government was just then having local difficulties with its Baltic port workers. The riots which were eventually to bring Gomulka down and put Giereck in power in Poland ruled out Gdynia for the Hilton assignment: it was no moment to be transporting weapons and explosives to the centre of the troubles.

Gregor suggested that the consignment might be shipped south-east down the Danube to the Romanian port of Constanta. This was less attractive, because to reach the Mediterranean, the dangerous cargo would have to sail from the Black Sea through the Bosphorus, under close surveillance from both the Russians and Turks. When the Romanian authorities mounted large-scale military manoeuvres early in January, a move in their ongoing chess game with the Soviet Union, Kent decided Constanta was unsuitable.

It would have to be Yugoslavia after all, and at least the expensive trial run had ironed out the difficulties. Kent now knew the consignment would have to go to Ploče because of the explosives. He knew a transit certificate was necessary, and, to reassure the jumpy Yugoslavs, a military escort for the trucks from the airport to the quayside. All this would need arranging and paying for. Gregor and Stefan would do the arranging. Kent would pay.

At the end of December 1970 Kent surveyed his work and found it good. Léon's team could be reactivated by a single telephone call. Jeff Thompson was reporting that the refit of Conquistador XIII was almost complete and the ship would be ready to sail to the Adriatic within a matter of days. A cable to Omnipol would, within a week, produce the arms at Ploče, ready for collection. All that remained was to fix the exact place and date of rendezvous for the package tour to Tripoli.

10 The Military Plan

The Hilton assignment was conceived as a detonator, an explosive charge to trigger off a chain reaction of revolt and bring Qadhafi down. Shalhi's sympathisers inside Libya were preparing the powder and awaited the spark which Léon and the team were to provide. For reasons of security Shalhi kept powder and spark rigidly separate at the planning stage. Just as he told no one in Libya the date or nature of the mercenary strike, so he withheld from his foreign friends the details of his follow-up plans for the coup. Kent was as much in his confidence as any foreigner could be, but even Kent learned only the broad outlines. It was a need-to-know situation. But at his many meetings with Bill and William, at constantly changing European places of rendezvous, Kent saw and heard enough to judge that Shalhi's intelligence from inside Libya was good.

Once, sometimes twice, a month couriers would meet Shalhi in German cities—before the massacre of Israeli athletes at the 1972 Munich Olympics, Arabs needed no visas for West Germany. These messengers travelled circuitously, usually via another Arab country, to bring him information by letter or, more commonly, by word of mouth. They carried back funds.

It was clear that Shalhi still had supporters in Tripoli—and not only in the prison. Many people in business, in the civil service, in the police, even in the army, were doing the same jobs as before Qadhafi's takeover, and among these some were prepared to risk their necks to bring about a counter-revolution. In a country so painfully short of skilled men, the regime could not afford to purge everyone of whose loyalty it was uncertain, and Qadhafi had not by 1971 won much popular support. He had seized power with a handful of associates, with whom he now ran Libya from behind the barbed-wire and machine guns of the Aziziya barracks. His power base was extremely narrow. This was Shalhi's asset. He judged it would take the defection of only one or two military and police units to strip his rival.

Kent was given a clue to Shalhi's thinking when, at different times in the run-up to the strike, Shalhi proposed that as well as breaking into the prison, the mercenaries should neutralise the barracks, seize the radio station or blow up the town's power supply. None of these suggestions attracted the planners. Knocking out the electricity generators, for example, was liable to be counter-productive, creating total confusion and making it that much more difficult for the counter-coup to establish itself afterwards. The radio station seemed a more tempting target until it was realised that the station was off the air in the decisive hours from 1 to 6 a.m., and, as all receivers would be switched off or tuned elsewhere, could make little contribution, one way or another, to

Shalhi's operation. By six o'clock the counter-coup would either have triumphed or failed.

As for the barracks, the planners were ready to defend themselves against interference from there, but were not geared to capture it. To land a force able to take on Qadhafi's army implied more money, more men, more boats, more logistical support, more trucks, the almost certain intervention of the great powers, and the loss of the Scarlet Pimpernel element of surprise. Surprise, and the confusion surprise would bring, were the planners' chief advantages, enough, they reckoned, to achieve their objective, the release of the political prisoners in the Hilton.

There is no foolproof blueprint for a *coup d'état*. No one could guarantee that Shalhi would at the end of the day emerge on top. But in a sense this did not affect the mercenaries: the team could go in, do their work and come out, even if no rising followed. A precisely defined military operation can be planned to the last detail, and the Hilton assignment was. Kent gave it nine chances out of ten of success.

Jeff Thompson's orders were to stay with Conquistador XIII on her voyage from Toulon, down the west coast of Italy, through the Straits of Messina, and up the Adriatic to Ploče. He was to take the arms and explosives on board, then turn south again for Sicily and collect the team and the principals from Catania, the port at the foot of Mount Etna on the island's east coast where he would leave the ship. Conquistador's next stop would be Tripoli.

This was no pleasure cruise. There was a lot to be done in the two days at sea. Only now would the squad of adventurous Frenchmen assembled by Léon be told their destination, briefed on their mission, drilled in specific tasks, and armed. Each man was instructed to travel to Catania in ordinary civilian clothes and bring with him a pair of soft-soled desert or rubber boots, dark-coloured slacks, shirt and pullover, a knife, fork and spoon, a mess-tin and mug. On board they would be issued with a sleeping bag, a webbing belt and ammunition pouches, a water bottle, torch, sheath knife and combat cap—in the melée ahead they would have to be able to identify each other. Each group of three men was to be given a compass.

The most lengthy task was to open the fifty-five crates picked up at Ploče, strip down each weapon, degrease and clean it, and assemble it ready for action, then test it by firing into the waves. When each man had been issued with his personal weapons, the rest of the arsenal was to be broken down into forty-five loads and packed into sacks and kitbags for distribution to the released prisoners. Two full magazines were to be attached to each weapon with masking tape. To speed up the laborious process of loading ammunition into the machine gun belts, Omnipol had supplied a belting machine.

The team would be split up into groups with different responsibilities. Three 'fire groups' of three men each were to provide cover during the operation, while a 'demolition group' breached the walls and a 'release group' rescued the prisoners. A 'diversion group' would lay mines and man anti-tank weapons and machine guns on the approach roads. On the voyage the demolition group's job was to test detonators, blasting fuse and exploders, and make ready the different charges for the outer, inner and internal walls. Two men were to stay on the beach to guard the landing craft and prepare for a quick getaway, and another two on board the ship·to make quite sure the captain did not abandon his passengers.

Stowed away in the hull of Conquistador were six Zodiac inflatable boats, a type of landing craft used by sophisticated armed forces for running up on to beaches. Powered by forty-horsepower outboard engines, they are twenty foot long and six foot wide, capable of carrying 5,000 pounds in weight. Accessories include two foot-operated bellows with connecting hosepipe, two paddles in case of emergency, a repair kit, and an unwinding wooden floor which goes down the middle like a duck-board. The Zodiacs were not considered a sinister element of Conquistador's cargo: more easily stowed than orthodox lifeboats or rafts, they are carried by many pleasure yachts nowadays. On the way from Toulon these had to be inflated and inspected and their engines test-run.

A vital drill was to familiarise the various groups with the communications equipment, the eight Tokai transceivers with which they would maintain contact with each other throughout, and the three Cossor sets for communications between mothercraft, Zodiacs and the shore. In addition, and quite apart from the ship's radio, there was equipment for a ship to shore radio link transmitting monosyllabic signals on a fixed frequency. The shore end of this link was to be carried by the advance party put into Libya to arrange for trucks to transport the team. This particular gadget, which to non-technical eyes seemed an ordinary wireless set, had been put together discreetly in a private workshop in the French provinces. It was reckoned that even if the Libyans had modern direction-finding equipment, they would be unlikely to pick up the ship's signal on a one-time basis. The men were instructed in a simple code as follows:

Hello 10 Boat all OK
Hello 20 Shore all OK
Hello 30 Total cancellation
Hello 24 Twenty-four hour delay
Hello 48 Forty-eight hour delay
Hello 72 Seventy-two hour delay

It was Léon's special concern to issue personal weapons and equipment to Bill and William, supervise their handling and testing of these weapons and test the loud-hailers which were to play a key part in the storming of the Hilton.

On the appointed night in early February 1971 Conquistador XIII was to sail into Libyan waters, heading for a beach fifteen miles east of Tripoli. For weeks the planners had scanned the calendar for moonless nights, then deciding that total darkness was as much a disadvantage as an advantage. Only the period of full moon would be avoided. A rigid timetable was to govern the approach.

2145 hours: Boat arrives sixteen nautical miles off the beach and proceeds at eight knots. Ship to shore radio link is opened for one minute in every five.

2245 hours: Boat arrives eight nautical miles off the beach. Speed reduced to four knots. Direction-

APPROACH TIMINGS & COMMS CODE	REMARKS
2145 hrs boat arrives 16 N. miles off of lido	open voice li[?] 1min every 5 m[?] for 1 hr
2145 - 2245hrs Sail at 8 Knots	
2245 hrs arrive 8 N. miles off of lido	open D.F link on for 30 sec off for 30 sec for 5 mins in every
2245 hrs ⎱ sail at 4 knots & place 2345 hrs ⎰ equip in seperate boatloads on deck	
2345 hrs boats launched & loaded	dependant on weat[?]
0015 hrs arrive 1-2 N.miles off lido & disembark party	
0015 hrs no D.F or wrls contact	Torch signals
0045 hrs arrive lido, make contact with beach party	
0115 hrs depart lido for hotel	journey 26 mins
0115 hrs No contact groups depart	repeat at 24 h[?] interval max 3 d[?]
0145 hrs arrive hotel	
0205 hrs depart hotel	
0235 hrs arrive lido & embark	
0250 hrs depart area	

Extract from military plan

finding link opened. Men carry up kitbags of arms and other equipment and stack them on deck in separate boatloads.

2345 hours: Zodiacs are launched and loaded.

0015 hours: Boat arrives one nautical mile off the beach and drops anchor. All lights extinguished. Men leave mothercraft for Zodiacs according to pre-arranged order. All direction-finding and wireless contact cut. Contact with beach party made by torch signals.

0045 hours: Men arrive beach.

The six Zodiacs were to run in, in diamond formation, their engines throttled back to eliminate noise if the state of the sea made this possible. In each craft, one member of the team would serve as cox. Léon and seven other mercenaries would ride in the first boat. Four of these would immediately fan out as sentries, two on the beach to the left and right of the landing, and two others to guard the trucks waiting by the edge of the road beyond the dunes. Léon's three remaining men were to form a central control group, checking with the truck drivers that all was quiet in Tripoli and along their route, and helping with the unloading and stacking of the equipment.

Bill and William and their escorts were to follow in the next two boats and go immediately to the trucks. The demolition group and its equipment would be loaded in the rear vehicle, the kitbags of spare weapons in the front one. All this had to be done in total silence on the desert-quiet beach.

Half an hour was considered long enough to get the men and weapons off the boats and into the trucks, but within this short span of time several possible

seen approaching lay down untill
they have passed, if given the
order to stop movement, wait
for the O.K from Control.
Do not join in any action at the
vehicles unless ordered.

Beach sentries orders

The most likely situation to
arise, is a customs patrol on
horseback, attention to the
killing of the horse is to take
priority, to stop it returning to
the stable, all riders to be
eliminated, rider & horse if
possible to be dragged into
the dunes if you can control
the situation info control at
the end of beach phase for
assistance in removing evidence.

Vehicle sentries

Responsible for stopping movement
of the equipment party on
the approach of enemy personnel

The most likely situation to
arise, is a normal visit through
curiosity of a single person, he
will be eliminated by one of
friends. If two or three people
approach friends will try to
draw them away from the
vehicles, when friend throws
himself flat this is the signal
for the sentry to open fire
plus assistance from friend

emergencies were foreseen. If a car passed along the road, the men had instructions to lie down and freeze all movement until the vehicle had gone by. A more sombre possibility was an interruption by a customs patrol. It was known that the beaches were occasionally checked by a lone mounted policeman armed with a rifle in a saddle holster. Instructions to the beach sentries were to shoot both horse and rider, giving priority to the horse to prevent it from galloping off to the stable and raising the alarm. After the killing, horse and rider were if possible to be dragged into the dunes.

What the planners feared above all else was that the unusual activity on the beach would attract the interest of a casual passer-by, perhaps a fisherman or a villager. If a single intruder was spotted, Bill or William was to greet him in Arabic and then their escort would eliminate him. If more than one appeared at the same time, the drill was for Bill or William to draw them away from the vehicles, then throw themselves flat. If the sentry felt he could not handle the situation alone, he was to call on his Tokai for reinforcements from the control group on the beach. All weapons to be used by the sentries on the beach and at the trucks were equipped with silencers. It was up to Léon to choose the right men for these nerve-racking tasks—extra cool and steady characters, not hotheads itching for a fight.

One of the most difficult problems was the provision of a beach party to meet the invading force. Trucks were needed to carry the team to their target, and it was recognised as psychologically desirable that these should be waiting for the mercenaries as they

Move to target

1. Vehicles to travel at 30 mph 50 yds apart

2. From beach to target takes 26 minutes

3. Beach to target route see sketch 25

4. Route through town to target see sketch 26

5. Elimination groups to sit by tail-board at rear of vehicle

6. Small observation slit to be cut in the front of the canopy

7. <u>Road blocks</u>
Are not expected, but! The possibility of a minor police check could occur. If this does occur, a friend in the cab of the vehicle will try to bluff it out, if the police insist on searching the vehicle, A friend will get out of the cab and slam the door hard, this is the signal for the elimination group to be prepared to kill the policeman debus and eliminate any others assisted by friend

8. <u>Arrival point</u>
Final road to debusing point is a slight downhill gradient, vehicles to approach as silently as possible and halt in the cover of a large overhanging tree, see sketch 26

landed: a welcome by their mates on the beach, and the assurance that the Libyans were not lined up and ready to take them on, would give morale a much needed fillip at this first anxious moment on enemy soil. But how was transport to be provided without confiding the date of the landing to *someone* at the Libyan end and thus endangering security? The planners settled for an elaborate two-phase operation.

It was arranged that a trusted contact in Tripoli would hire two trucks from a small haulage company. The contact was told that they were to be used one night to carry a load of smuggled wines and spirits to a secret warehouse in dry Libya. Standard five-ton vehicles were specified, with a tarpaulin cover and rear flap which could be lifted to allow the men to jump out quickly. The trucks were to be left, with ignition keys in place, in a quiet road on the outskirts of the town where the 'smugglers' would collect them. At the same time three French mercenaries were to hire a car in Tunis, drive across the frontier to Tripoli (under the guise of travel agents surveying Libya's tourist potential), take possession of the parked trucks and drive them to the beach.

The only compromising equipment the Frenchmen were to carry with them was the radio set capable of transmitting to the ship. The set was stripped down and the parts carefully concealed in camera tripods and shaving kits. All that a customs official would see was a conventional portable radio, too old and battered to be worth appropriating. To check on arrangements and locate the beach, the three men were to arrive in Tripoli two or three days before the assault and be told the exact night by an apparently innocent telephone call from Europe. It was foreseen that they might be set in motion, rumble down to the beach and find no landing party there because of some last minute delay. In that event, they were to return on the following two nights, wait at the beach and signal out to sea from 2145 hours, when Conquistador should be ready to pick up their signals, to 0115 hours. Then, if nothing happened, they were to go away.

When contact was made, the drivers were to hand over their two trucks to Léon, arm themselves with submachine guns and incendiary grenades, and set off in their hired car on a specific mission of their own. Their job was to distract attention from the scene of the main action by creating as much disturbance as they could. Two petrol stations a mile or so from the Hilton had been located, and these were to be attacked with grenades and set on fire, causing their underground containers, each of over a thousand gallons, to explode. The explosions were timed to take place within minutes of the breaching of the prison walls, in the hope that the more spectacular petrol station fires would draw off troops from the barracks and divide the enemy ranks. The incendiarists were then to race to the Hilton to reinforce Léon's team.

The climax to the months of preparation, to the slow stealthy approach by sea, to the laborious build up of men and equipment on the beach was to be a brutal twenty minutes of action, sandwiched between a twenty-six minute journey there and a twenty-six minute journey back. All in all, the round trip from beach to Hilton was scheduled to take an hour and

twenty minutes, allowing eight minutes for contingen-
cies. The 'sharp end' was pared down to the last
minute.

At 0115 hours the car and the two trucks were to
leave in convoy for the town, travelling at a modest
thirty miles per hour, with the vehicles fifty yards
apart. Bill in the cab of the first truck, and William in
the cab of the second, would direct the drivers.

It is not unusual for a truck to come into Tripoli
late at night on the Benghazi road; in summer drivers
go by night for the greater coolness. So even at one in
the morning, two vehicles with local number plates
were not expected to attract attention. But one could
not be too careful. To allow the men huddled in the
back to spot trouble before it hit them, a small
observation slit was to be cut in the front of each
canopy. In each vehicle two men were detailed as an
'elimination group' to sit by the tail-board with
silenced 7.65 mm pistols and knives at the ready.

Reconnaissance had shown that the route through
the outskirts of the town to the Hilton was free of
road blocks, but the convoy would have to pass an
ordnance depot on the right of the road and two
small police posts, nine kilometres apart, on the left.
Each of these posts was slightly off the road and
would house about ten men, most of them asleep at
this hour. They sometimes checked traffic, however,
and there was always the entirely unforeseeable
incident—the challenge from an officious policeman
at a traffic light, even the risk of a road accident.

The drill in such an event was that Bill or William
would try to bluff it out in Arabic from the window
of the cab: there was some reluctance to kill

policemen, regarded as sympathetic to the old regime. But if the police insisted on searching the vehicle, the elimination group would be prepared to leap out and dispose of the opposition as swiftly and quietly as possible. The signal to launch the elimination group into action was to be the slamming of the cab door.

A mile from the prison the car leading the convoy was to split off and head for the targeted petrol pumps. The two trucks would continue on their way, freewheeling silently down the last incline towards the Hilton, and coming to a halt in the cover of a large overhanging tree across the street from the north-west corner of the prison walls.

The west wall was chosen as the focus of the attack. This was the rear wall, furthest away from the gates, the guardroom and the armoured cars. Even before the trucks had stopped, two men were to leap out and run to sentry positions at either end of the wall, some two hundred yards apart. If a prison guard happened to be looking over the wall at that highly compromising moment, they had to pick him off. Thereafter their job was to halt any hostile movement down the approach roads to the west wall.

Only from Qadhafi's stronghold, the Aziziya barracks some three kilometres west of the prison, was real opposition expected. The tanks and armoured cars stationed there would no doubt be mobilised once the alarm was given, but even in a first-class army it takes some twenty minutes to assemble a crew and start up an armoured vehicle. In Libya, the attackers reckoned, it would take longer. They would benefit from the confusion. The attackers knew what they were doing, the Libyans would take time to adjust. But the guard commander at the Hilton was bound to telephone Aziziya, and sooner or later reinforcements would be on their way. A heavily armed diversion group was to be sent to wait for them. It would lay anti-personnel mines and prepare anti-tank positions on both sides of the road from the barracks.

The next four men out of the truck were drawn from the fire groups and would be carrying light aluminium scaling ladders. They were to be the sharp-shooters, the first to storm up the outer wall, eliminate any visible sentries on the inner wall catwalk, then cut their way through the barbed-wire apron. John Brooke Miller had reported after his reconnaissance in Tripoli a fact later confirmed, that the night watch on the catwalk took over at 2145 hours, at which time the engines of the armoured cars in the prison were also warmed up. By 0145, four hours later, the engines would be cold and the six-man patrol at its lowest ebb and probably dozing in corner pill-boxes. Libyan sentries were not much used to being disturbed by an inspecting officer in the middle of the night.

Next over, through the gap in the wire, would be the rest of the three fire groups led by Léon, bringing a ladder with them. Their task was to scale the outer wall, race across the strip of garden, then climb the inner wall on to the catwalk, and from there on to the roof of the cell blocks. Well spread out and with massive fire power, they could dominate the whole prison, containing any movement in the internal courtyards or in the garden area between the inner and outer walls. In particular they had to immobilise the armoured cars, a vulnerable target in an enclosed space, and prevent any attempt by the Libyan guards to break out in force from the guardroom by the main gate. The mercenaries were not an assassination squad: they would kill if they had to, but their weapons were to discourage resistance. They were not expecting any heroics in return, and an occasional burst of gunfire was judged enough to persuade the Libyans to keep their heads down. The average soldier has no inclination to stick his neck out when firing is going on outside.

Number two fire group was specially detailed to provide covering fire for the three-man release group, led by Shalhi himself, which would be the third lot over the wall. Protected from the roof, they were to climb down into the central courtyard of the prison and blow open selected cell doors with small plastic charges prepared on the voyage. For Shalhi, this would be his finest hour. Shouting through the loud-hailer, he was to announce his presence to prisoners and guards, telling the first to get ready for the break-out and the second that they would come to no harm if they stayed indoors and laid down their weapons. 'This is Umar al-Shalhi speaking! The police and army have come over to the liberation forces! The tyrant Qadhafi has fallen! . . .'

Shalhi had to work fast. He had not only to rouse and rally the dazed prisoners, shaken awake by the firing, but to pump them full of courage and prepare them for further action in the town. He would have to tell them that weapons were waiting for them outside. The regime in the Hilton was humane—at least for political prisoners, who wore their own

Position of ladders in relation to breech

not to scale measurements approximate

N

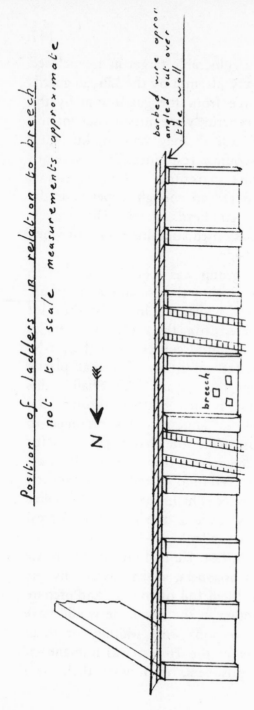

barbed wire apron angled out over the wall

breech

1) Buttresses protrude 6"
2) 14 foot between each buttress
3) Wall is rendered with cement-
4) Length of wall 200 yards
5) Breach position between the 11th and 12th buttress from the North

clothes, ate food brought them daily by their relatives, were allowed visitors, books and newspapers. But a long period of incarceration, however unrigorous, saps a man's spirit as well as his strength, and by this time the prisoners would have been confined for seventeen months. Inevitably their reactions would be slow, and perhaps some, fearful of what they were being let in for, would prefer to close their ears and remain under their beds. At least half the political prisoners were police and army officers of the former regime, who were no strangers to weapons. It was on these that Shalhi was counting for active support.

By this time the Hilton would have been rocked by two large explosions. While the first wave of mercenaries was scaling the outer wall, the demolition group would be hurriedly unloading its equipment, wall charges and initiation sets at the north-west corner of the prison. The perimeter wall of the Hilton is rendered with cement and strengthened every fourteen feet by a buttress. Between the eleventh and twelfth buttresses, counting from the north, was the spot chosen for the breach. In a matter of seconds the demoliton experts would have unreeled the firing cable to the breach position and fixed three ten-pound centre-primed plastic charges to the wall, propping them on broom handles wedged into the ground. On the first sound of firing from inside the prison, the charge would be initiated. The explosives were to be carefully weighed and sited to make a breach seven foot six inches long by six foot high.

When the dust had settled, the group would rush through the hole and repeat the process against the

Attachment of inner & outer wall charges

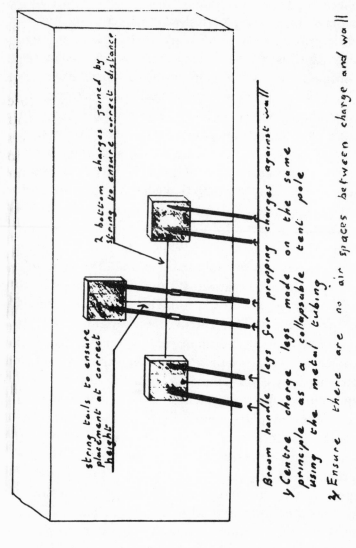

2 bottom charges joined by string to ensure correct distance

string tails to ensure placement at correct height

Broom handle legs for propping charges against wall

y Centre charge legs made on the same principle as a collapsable tent pole using the metal tubing

y Ensure there are no air spaces between charge and wall

inner wall. This led into the cells. To avoid blowing up Shalhi's friends in their beds, the demolition group was to make the second breach into the washrooms. Once in they would blow the doors into the central yard and into the adjoining cell blocks with two-pound plastic charges in which magnets had been moulded to hold them against the locks.

The whole series of explosions, each taking only a couple of minutes to complete, would leave a jagged, dusty corridor from the centre of the prison to the outside world. The corridor was not to get the mercenaries in, but the prisoners out, for it was not thought likely that dozens of newly released detainees could easily escape by ladder. The signal for the general exit would be given by the release group firing a Verey pistol from the roof. With the fire groups still providing cover, the prisoners would then be hustled out to where William was waiting to arm them by the breach in the outer wall.

At once Léon would call in his mercenaries, check them as they came through the main breach with their dead and wounded (for this was not an operation in which an injured mercenary could be left behind), and despatch them in a body to the trucks. Casualties were estimated at under twenty per cent—three or four men killed or wounded scaling the walls or igniting the charges. Last to embark would be the petrol station incendiarists, whose hired car was to be left at the prison, the diversion group summoned by Tokai, and finally the sentries.

The released prisoners would thus be left to conquer Tripoli with no transport except one car and whatever vehicles they could fortuitously acquire.

But distances in Tripoli are not great and there was more preparedness among Shalhi's supporters in the town than the mercenaries were aware of. The explosion would be a signal for these supporters to move on certain positions which could then be stiffened with the machine guns and anti-tank weapons the team had brought in. A number of police posts had been earmarked for takeover, as well as several police armouries.

Their job done, the team was to drive back to the beach, still at a sober thirty miles per hour in order not to attract attention. Léon and his second-in-command Jules would now take the places of Bill and William next to the drivers, ready to jump out and go into violent action if challenged. On arrival at the beach the vehicles would be searched to ensure that no evidence of their use remained to get their owner into trouble, and then simply abandoned.

Guided to the landingcraft by one of the coxes left in charge of them, the men would embark at speed and head for Conquistador XIII with Léon in the control boat. If they had trouble finding the mothercraft, still anchored without lights, they were to raise a radar reflector and ask for directions over the Cossor link.

Once aboard and the landingcraft hauled up, the anchor would be weighed and Conquistador set full steam ahead for the open sea before first light. But it was not yet time to relax: there was still the possibility of pursuit and search. Only when the ship was well away from Libyan waters could the men carefully set about destroying all traces of their night's work.

Arms, equipment and unused ammunition were to be tied to the unwanted landingcraft whose air compartments would be slashed before being pitched overboard. Special attention was to be paid to cleaning the ship of any sand that might have been brought on board. The ship would then be searched minutely. Any man found in possession of any operational equipment would forfeit his pay.

11 The Man from the SIS

At the best of times Jeff Thompson had a low gravelly voice, all the grittier on the crackling long-distance telephone lines from some little harbourside bistro in Toulon. James Kent, receiving regular reports on the progress of Conquistador's refit, could visualise Jeff's impassive English presence looking distinctly out of place in his lively Mediterranean setting. By nature and by habit Jeff was laconic. 'No sweat,' he would reply to Kent's queries, or sometimes, 'No problem.' As the weeks passed this became *'Pas de problème.'*

He had been a long time away from base and was manifesting a certain erosion of his Englishness. After twenty years of beer-drinking British soldiering, he now found himself drinking wine and smoking Gauloises. Never having had much to do with boats before, he was learning nautical terms for the first time—but in French, and since he did not know the English equivalents, his conversation was sprinkled with *beauprés* and *tribords, soupapes de sûreté* and *pompes à vapeur.*

Basically Jeff was a good warrant officer, thoroughly dependable when in place in the pyramid of command but not used to working on his own for any length of time without the reassurance of authority. His solitude, the unfamiliarity of France, the long drawn out suspense of the Hilton assignment all began to prey on his mind, and his nerves were in a ragged state when at Christmas 1970 he had to take time off for Conquistador's refit and go alone into Libya for a last survey of the arrangements for the strike.

Shalhi and William had been much impressed by what they had seen of him at Bari and were aware that the detailed military planning probably owed more to him than to John Brooke Miller. It was on their insistence that Jeff was selected for the final reconnaissance.

Apart from the continuing flow of information from Shalhi's couriers, checks had been made on different aspects of the plan by European emissaries. Steve Reynolds had been into Tripoli with his wife and had verified the distances involved, but Kent found his information incomplete. A member of the French team went to Tunisia to run through the routine of hiring a car there and driving into Libya. It was a useful exercise because he met with unexpected difficulties. The Tunisian hire company had recently had two cars impounded in Libya, and it took a day or two of negotiation for the Frenchman to restore their confidence. In Libya he spent the best part of a night on the beach east of Tripoli and observed no one except in the distance a solitary policeman on horseback. As D-Day approached Jeff was to be sent in order that his trained military eye might spot any remaining weak links.

He had a relative in Rhodesia whom he wanted to visit at Christmas before making the Libyan reconnaissance. Perhaps he imagined that, if the Libyans had wind of the Hilton assignment, he would be safer coming in from the south than from Europe. In any event, on his way back from Salisbury he got as far as Tunis, in some doubt about the wisdom of what he was going to do.

Jeff had no intelligence background. He was not hardened to clandestinity or trained for the loneliness of the undercover agent. In a group of three, or even two, he was unflappable; alone he was just one big anxiety. The conviction grew on him that his security had been blown to the Libyans, that they knew of his connection with Shalhi. It is curious how guilt in the mind can cause a man to interpret the most banal features of his environment as sinister, the look on the face of the hotel concierge, the touts in the lobby, a car moving out from the kerb behind his taxi.

The night before Jeff was due to cross the frontier into Libya, he was having a solitary drink in a bar of his Tunis hotel. When the waiter put a whisky and soda on the table at his elbow, Jeff noticed a magazine lying there open at a page of advertising. Someone had scribbled across it with a biro. He looked closer and read the single word 'Tripoli' followed by an exclamation mark. Below it was a doodle which to his startled eye looked like a diagram of part of the prison. This was clearly some sort of warning message put there for him to see. His hair stood on end.

The next morning Kent in Frankfurt received a

cryptic telegram from Tunisia. It read: 'Cancel all my holiday arrangements will meet you as arranged,' and was signed 'J Goring.' Kent could make little sense of it, but recognised that it meant bad news. Twenty-four hours later a deeply disturbed Jeff reached Frankfurt with the confession that he just could not go through with his mission. Under the burden of living with a problem too long, this cool, tough soldier had cracked.

Kent had promised an up-to-the-minute report by Jeff on the situation in Libya, and Shalhi had come specially to Frankfurt to hear it. At that very moment he was waiting, no doubt impatiently, in the splendid presidential suite on the twentieth floor of the Intercontinental Hotel. Four floors lower down the building, in a smaller suite, Kent considered the position. It was a moment of crisis. If Jeff, whom the principals admired, was now throwing in the sponge, what confidence could they have in the rest of the operation? Kent took Jeff out and for nearly three hours walked him up and down by the river Main, explaining, cajoling, persuading, reassuring. Of course the assignment had not been blown. This time the planning had gone like clockwork, everything was poised for the strike. All that was required to guarantee success was one last on the spot check by one of the authors of the military plan. Jeff's fears were groundless, the delusions of a man unused to secret operations. In Tunisia he had been absolutely clean, without a shred of compromising evidence on him. As for the so-called warning which had driven him out of his wits, it was obviously a meaningless scribble by some English or American oil technician,

in Tunis for a weekend of drink and relaxation from
the prohibition and puritanism of Libya.

Jeff recovered his nerve. The next day he left for
Geneva to pick up a direct flight for Tripoli. His
reconnaissance was faultless. He checked routes,
distances, timing, angles of fire. He counted
buttresses on the prison wall and verified the location
of the petrol stations to be set alight and the exact
position of the landing beach. He made contact with
Shalhi's Arab link, each man identifying himself by
matching the torn halves of a one-dollar bill, and
stayed to test the drill for the trucks. Sure enough,
they were there, on the outskirts of the town, with
the keys in the cab. After reporting all clear to Kent
and the principals, he rejoined Conquistador XIII.

Good at reassuring others, Kent had no one to
reassure him. The weight of responsibility, the strain
of constant travel, the need for elementary but
time-consuming security measures were beginning to
wear him down. Most of his time was being spent
outside Britain. He worked till late at night and woke
again at five to make the routine telephone checks
round Europe. Between five and seven in the morning
is about the only time of day when European
telephone lines are free and one can be certain of
finding people at home. An alternative is to telephone
after midnight, but at that hour one risks ruining
someone's night's sleep. Arabs tend to waken early,
and Kent's principals far preferred an early morning
call. So Kent was on the phone at dawn almost every
day. More precious to him than sleep was a telephone
he could dial himself, without the risk and the tedium
of going through an operator. He carried in his head

the codes for Frankfurt, Hamburg, Munich, Vienna, Paris, Geneva. 'What's happening to the boat in Toulon? How is Gregor making out in Prague? Has Léon any problems? What about the guy we sent into Tripoli? What's the latest intelligence from the other side.' These were the questions, phrased in veiled language, to which he wanted answers.

He knew himself well and had devised his own therapies against depression and breakdown. When he sensed exhaustion gaining on him, he switched off for a day or two and disappeared. He became a connoisseur of the luxury hide-outs of the European rich. Over the weeks from mid-November 1970 to the end of January 1971, he escaped three times, to the Austrian ski resort Bad Gastein, to Venice for forty-eight hours of total idleness and a first night at the Teatro di Fenice, and to Monte Carlo. Here on New Year's Day 1971 Léon sought him out.

The Frenchman was beginning to grow restive. Forced into inaction, he had done some thinking. He had never been told in so many words that the country to be attacked was Libya, and in all the plans the target was indicated simply as 'the hotel.' But Léon had his political wits about him. He may have thought the objective was to be a Greek island, and the prisoners to be freed the opponents of the Greek colonels' military dictatorship. But now he wanted certainty. There is a break-even point in a mercenary's mind. He has to weigh the risks against the rewards and judge for himself whether the odds are in his favour. The longer action was delayed, the greater grew the security risk and the more information Léon demanded to make sure he was not

leading his men into a trap. Kent told him they were
bound for Libya.

Léon was not an expert in counter-espionage, but
he could not afford to ignore its implications. After
all his life depended on it. To sort out the significance
of what Kent had told him he needed help. As a
mercenary of numerous campaigns he naturally had
his contacts inside SDECE, the *Service de documen-
tation extérieure et de contre-espionnage*, France's
CIA. In his own quiet way Léon now plugged into
SDECE for intelligence cover.

Kent was not sorry to take Léon into his
confidence. He had liked and trusted the team leader
from the beginning, and now that neither John Miller
nor Jeff Thompson was intending to go with the mercenaries into Tripoli, it was desirable to have Léon fully
briefed, politically as well as militarily. But Kent did
not tell him that Umar al-Shalhi was the principal.

Shalhi too was having his problems. Balking at the
vast sums which they were being asked to pay for his
abduction, the Libyans had decided to harry him
rather than capture him. In the conviction that he
was dangerous to them, they had approached the
Swiss authorities to circumscribe his activities as a
political exile. The Swiss are hospitable to wealthy
fugitives but they are sensitive to the abuse of the
haven they offer. 'Distinguished visitors' are often
requested to sign an undertaking not to engage in
political activities on Swiss soil. Anxious not to
offend his hosts, Shalhi observed his pledge and
thereafter conducted his secret business from Austria
and West Germany.

So Kent had to include German cities on his

itinerary. He would meet Shalhi at the Vierjahrezeiten at Hamburg or the Continental at Munich, in airport hotels or in Shalhi's own Vienna apartment. Once in a departure lounge they saw each other by chance. Shalhi, accompanied by a stunningly beautiful, expensively dressed young woman, brushed past him with a murmured 'You don't know me.' By this time Shalhi and Kent were on terms of mutual trust. If one were dispirited and felt himself drifting in the dark, the other would cheer him up.

Shalhi could be overbearing and impatient, displaying a lordly disregard of detail. Casually he mentioned one day that his brother Abd al-Aziz had some time before been moved to a different cell in the Hilton, one near the guardroom, the point of maximum danger. Kent was extremely angry. Did Shalhi not realise that this would mean a change in the military plan, the redefinition of the deployment of the release group? But Shalhi was not a man to take reproaches humbly. Kent took to using William to put the more routine things over in Arabic to Umar, but there was a gap between the two Arabs, and Kent could not be sure that all his messages were passed on.

On 7 January 1971 Kent arrived in Vienna to brief Shalhi and William on the complex details of the redrawn military plan. Their crucial task that day was to fix the date of the strike. As on a similar occasion in Geneva three months previously, they decided to time it for one month ahead. Of the irreducible three components of the operation, the team was more or less under starter's orders, the boat was almost ready to sail from Toulon, and the arms had been ordered—but not yet fully paid for or delivered. This was a loose end Kent had to tie up himself.

Meeting up with Gregor and Stefan in Vienna, Kent left for Czechoslovakia in a rented Mercedes on Sunday, 10 January. At the border the exuberant Stefan produced from the boot of the car a carrier-bag loaded with cartons of American cigarettes, a bottle of whisky, chocolates, and half a dozen pairs of nylon tights. The Mercedes was waved into Czechoslovakia with broad smiles.

As usual Gregor was less sanguine than his companion. He had not been told about the operation, and now, when he was beginning to suspect that this was no ordinary commercial arms deal, he did not want to be told. As far as he was concerned, it was a transaction to be effected legally and as expeditiously as possible. But he was tactful as always, and seeing Kent was under pressure, forbore to thrust his own anxieties on him. 'Give me the good news first,' Kent told him wearily. This time there was the good news that Gregor had been able to secure a room at the Yalta Hotel in Prague. It was not Gregor's fault that three of the hotel's four boilers had broken down on Christmas Day, leaving the kitchen the only comfortable place. With Prague in the grip of winter and the temperature indoors at one degree below zero, Kent strode around in his sheepskin coat failing to keep warm.

His first call on Monday morning was at the Omnipol offices at 11 Washintonova Street, a short distance from the hotel in Wenceslas Square. Here, flanked by the ever-attentive Gregor and Stefan, he checked on the order, added a few items, established that CSA were once again prepared to lay on a freight plane to Yugoslavia, made sure that the Czechs were obtaining the necessary transit permit from the Yugoslav authorities. He got an undertaking from Omnipol that once the sum owing was paid, the arms would be flown to Split, the nearest airport to Ploče, within seven days. For extra assurance, Gregor arranged dinner and a social evening to ease the passing of the order through the bureaucratic machine.

From now on developments picked up pace. One after another the different cogs in Kent's carefully constructed engine started to turn at the appointed times in their appointed places, and in the third week of January 1971 the Hilton assignment began to roll in earnest.

The time had come to summon the men most directly involved to an operational briefing. So far Kent had been the only link between the different participants. Now they must be brought together to be forged into a fighting instrument.

Where could they meet discreetly but comfortably? Kent thought of Deauville, or better still, the château hotel perched at the top of the charming little town of Montreuil-sur-mer, half an hour's drive from Le Touquet, and asked his secretary in London to make the arrangements. She was unlucky. Deauville had put up its expensive shutters for the winter, while the proprietors of the château were taking a month off. With sinking heart Kent learned that the group was booked in at Abbeville in the flat, dreary, gastronomically undistinguished Pas de Calais.

In the second-class hotel, the mercenaries looked

like a conference of unusually tough pyramid salesmen. Léon brought with him not only Jules but also the leaders of the fire, release and diversion groups and his chief explosives expert. With the captain of Conquistador XIII, Jeff came up from Toulon, producing for the benefit of the hotel restaurant a ready-knotted tie which fastened with a clip to the collar of his shirt, transforming his appearance in a moment from that of an informal adventurer to that of a solidly respectable citizen. Kent arrived alone.

Together the men went through the military plan, checking that each knew his role. They were not there to rehearse the strike—men with well practised military skills do not need rehearsal; indeed rehearsal can be a disadvantage in coping with the uncertainties of battle—but to allocate responsibilities. Problems of control in action hardly arose as the mercenaries would be equipped with walkie-talkies and never further than a hundred yards from the centre of the operation. The main purpose of the Abbeville meeting was to bring home to the men their interdependence.

One strain in the structure of command soon showed itself. It became apparent at Abbeville that the captain of the ship, a congenital grumbler, did not consider himself under Léon's orders. Faced with this evidence that his first uneasiness about the captain was only too well-founded, Kent realised that a mistake had been made in not thoroughly integrating the crew into the assignment from the beginning. On this job they were not ordinary sailors, but sailors virtually at war, liable to be strafed from the air or intercepted at sea on the voyage back. As such, they should be under the same strict discipline as the team. The problem was temporarily solved when Léon took the captain aside and brutally outlined what might happen to him if he did not co-operate. But these threats only postponed a permanent solution.

From Abbeville, the conference scattered on January 19—Léon and Jules to their homes in Paris where they were to remain on the alert for the word to entrain with the rest of the team for Catania; Jeff and the captain to Toulon with orders to set sail at once, taking four mercenaries with them to test the Zodiacs; Kent to London to arrange for daily contact to be made with the ship. He took a flat in Princes Gate, near the Albert Hall—and even nearer the Libyan embassy, just forty yards along the road—and installed a man there to take Jeff's telephone calls from successive ports round the coast of Italy. At Genoa bad weather caused a temporary hold-up, then Conquistador steamed swiftly onwards, turning the heel of Italy to reach Brindisi on January 25.

But the captain remained a constant aggravation. Each day Jeff had further trouble to report—demands for extra money, forebodings about Conquistador's performance, threats to ditch the assignment. Losing patience at last, Léon flew to Brindisi and dismissed the captain on the spot. It irked Léon to pay him at all, but to ensure the captain's silence, payment at a future date had to be guaranteed. Léon had brought to Italy a personally chosen replacement, a seasoned sailor who understood the kind of exploit he was being invited to join and who agreed that, except in matters of navigation, he would submit to Léon's

authority. Having impressed upon the crew the fact
that he was boss, Léon returned to Paris.

Meanwhile on 21 January, Kent met Gregor in
Geneva to hand over the balance of Omnipol's money
which Gregor carried to Prague with a request to set
the consignment moving immediately. By the 27th
the arms and explosives would be at Ploče.

With twelve days to go to the climax of the
assignment on February 6, one thing remained to be
done. Kent needed to establish an operational
headquarters where he could maintain control of
communications while the beach party moved into
Tripoli at the same time as Conquistador XIII took
Shalhi, William and the mercenaries aboard and
zeroed in on target. He needed somewhere within
telephone reach of London, Ploče, Catania, Tunis—
and Tripoli. He chose Naples. Two trusted women
assistants were sent from London to the Excelsior
Hotel, Naples, to man the telephone in shifts.

Kent left for Yugoslavia on his last trip before the
assignment went into action. He had to make sure
beyond possibility of error that Omnipol had
delivered the goods and that this time the Yugoslavs
would raise no obstacle to their smooth transit.

Ploče lies exactly 110 kilometres north of
Dubrovnik, exactly 110 kilometres south of Split.
Wishing to avoid the scene of the earlier débâcle,
Kent chose to stay at the attractive little port of
Split, where on arrival he was met by Gregor. From
there on 27 January they travelled to Ploče, checked
that the precious crates were indeed in the customs
shed, saw the commandant in charge of the harbour
and his customs staff. Then Gregor distributed several

twenty-dollar bills between them to encourage maximum efficiency. If anything were to go wrong, if urgent communications had to be made, at least the men at Ploče would be on their side. On Thursday 28 January Kent took the one flight a week to Rome, hired a car and drove down the autostrada to Naples and his headquarters in the Excelsior Hotel.

And there he found trouble.

The worried women in charge of the centre met him with the news that Jeff's nerve appeared to be cracking. He had been on the telephone almost every hour, sounding increasingly excited. He desperately wanted to speak to Kent. Something very strange indeed was happening at Bari.

Kent had one of the women telephone at once asking Jeff to call him back from a pay phone. When he did so fifteen minutes later, Kent, through a haze of anxiety and guarded language, began to put together the pieces of the story.

Conquistador had put in at Bari two days earlier, ready to cross to Ploče and pick up the arms on Wednesday, but there had been engine trouble and a day had been wasted putting it right. Then Jeff noticed that the Italian police had begun to take an interest in him and the ship. Every time he or one of the mercenaries or a member of the crew left Conquistador, they were shadowed by plainclothes men. The police had inquired about him at his hotel, he discovered, and in the morning two men had been waiting for him in the lobby, and had stuck so close to him all day that he was constantly bumping into them. At first it was something of a joke, leading them on a wildgoose chase round Bari, but when he started to think about it, it was not so funny. The Italians were obviously on to something and had decided to lean heavily on Conquistador. It seemed a deliberately clumsy attempt to warn off Jeff and his friends.

And that was not the end of it. That very morning the police had come on board, checked the papers of the ship and crew and conducted a thorough search. There was nothing to find, but the climate was becoming very hostile and unhealthy, and he did not like it at all.

Kent did some quick thinking. In a small place like Bari, the fighting silhouette of the ex-patrol boat could have aroused official curiosity. Conquistador XIII certainly did not much look like a pleasure craft or a freighter, and the police might well have wondered what she and her over large crew were up to. Kent also knew that security was by this time imperfect. Léon knew the destination, and one or two other members of the team and crew, including the captain, might have made an intelligent guess. An immediate change of scenery was necessary.

Cooling Jeff down as best he could, he instructed him to move the boat up to Trieste, a much larger port where Conquistador would be less conspicuous. This would give the captain a chance to test the engines and the general running of the ship, and the crew something to occupy their minds while they waited for the signal to sail to Ploče. It would also give Kent time to think. As in most countries, the police forces in Italy are organised on regional lines, so that what happened in Bari need not necessarily be known in Trieste. Kent hoped that once

Conquistador sailed out of the harbour at Bari, the authorities would forget her.

Although he liked to live adventurously, Jeff was essentially a law-abiding man, who had been formed by the closed system of the British army and did not want to put himself beyond any pale. To be followed like a criminal, even by the Italians, filled him with anguish. But Kent's soothing words worked.

Feeling that he had perhaps overreacted to the Italian threats and made a fool of himself, he returned to his hotel to sleep it off, ready to sail for Trieste the next morning, Friday 29 January. He was surprised by a knock on his door at 7.30 a.m., and even more surprised when his visitor turned out to be a stern looking Englishman formally clad in dark suit and trilby and carrying a rolled umbrella.

He came from London, or said he did (although it is more likely that he belonged to the British embassy in Rome), and implied that he represented the Ministry of Defence or the Secret Intelligence Service, or both.

'We know what you're up to. You're a bit old for this lark, aren't you?'

Jeff's world rocked. He managed a stuttered, 'What do you mean?'

The stranger's answer was to recite Jeff's army record with a precision which pointed indubitably to inside information. 'If you're in any doubt about what we know about you,' he went on mercilessly, 'listen to this.' And he reeled off confidential details about Jeff's family and next of kin. 'You know you shouldn't be here, Mr Thompson. It could be very unpleasant for you if you carry on with it.'

That was enough for Jeff. He crumbled. Twenty years of ingrained reverence for British authority could not be defied. Now certain that he was under the closest and most hostile surveillance, he did not dare use the telephone. In extreme agitation he rushed to the Hertz office at Bari, hired a car, sped to the harbour to tell the captain to proceed without him to Trieste, and then, as if the devil were on his trail, screeched out of town on the road to Naples. He arrived at the operational headquarters a demoralised man.

12 Power Games

President Nasser died suddenly on 28 September 1970. The removal of this towering piece from the Arab chessboard altered the prospects for every other player—not least for Umar al-Shalhi and his associates in the Hilton assignment. So long as Nasser lived, and even when his stature was diminished by defeat in the 1967 war, he dominated the Middle East scene, a monument in whose shadow other Arab personalities seemed puny figures. As a result, for the first twelve months of Qadhafi's regime Libya was still an unremarkable provincial outpost and the young colonel a johnny-come-lately distinguished chiefly by the fervour of his admiration for the heroic Nasser of his youth. But with the master gone, the disciple stepped forward to attempt to fill his place. Perhaps the biggest regret Shalhi had was not to have been able to strike in that first year, when his target was still of little importance to anyone.

When on 8 November 1970 Umar al-Shalhi and James Kent met in Geneva to relaunch the Hilton assignment after the first failure at Bari, events which were vitally to affect their plans were taking place in another part of the world. On the very same day in

Cairo, President Sadat, Colonel Qadhafi and President
Nimairi of the Sudan announced their intentions for a
tripartite union (from which the Sudan was
subsequently to withdraw, leaving Egypt and Libya in
each other's embrace). The first of September 1973
was fixed as the date for the fusion of the two
countries into a single state.

Not surprisingly these moves alerted the world.
Every chancellory, commentator, specialist on Middle
East affairs speculated about the consequences.
Would the young Qadhafi live to rule in Cairo over an
Arab empire? What would this seventh century
puritan do with his mountain of twentieth century
money? Was his fantasy world of backward-looking
religious extremism coming true? Qadhafi seemed
seriously to believe in Arab reconquest, not only of
Jerusalem and the whole of Palestine, but of every
position lost by Islam to the infidel from Uganda to
the Philippines. A leading Muslim divine, Shaikh
Mahmud Subhi, promised that Muslim civilisation
would spread from Libya 'to disperse the darkness of
materialism that is engulfing this world.' Clearly there
was going to be some action.

Instead of an attack on an obscure jail, which
Shalhi could reasonably have hoped would escape
international notice, he was now undertaking his
strike against a target lit by a blaze of publicity. In
particular he must count Egypt's formidable intelligence service among his enemies. The protection of
Qadhafi, the one man who could deliver Libya to the
Egyptians, had become the first priority of Cairo's
external policy.

Which among the bigger powers now taking a new

look at Libya would Shalhi and his associates have to
reckon as enemies—and which as friends? Where in
particular did Britain and America stand in the
line-up? Was there anything here he could turn to
advantage?

In spite of Britain's reluctance to see its nationals
involved, the signals from Whitehall spelled out thinly
disguised hostility to Qadhafi.

Not only had he taken over British Petroleum,
Barclays Bank and the British base, but in a series of
dramatic escapades he seemed to be waging global
war on the United Kingdom. He propped up Malta's
premier Dom Mintoff in the long wrangle with
Whitehall. He pledged arms and money to the IRA.
He forced down a BOAC airliner, and arrested and
later sent to their death two Sudanese Communists
on their way home to take over from the temporarily
deposed Nimairi. Later, he pumped funds into the
Ugandan dictatorship of General Idi Amin who
unleashed his thousands of unwanted Asians on
Britain in 1972.

Little wonder that Qadhafi got a bad press in
England where he was depicted as reactionary,
irresponsible, hysterical—if not downright mad. His
repeated disappearances were taken as evidence of
nervous breakdowns, in which he was reported to be
raving in his office, sedated and strait-jacketed in a
hospital, or simply deposed. (In fact Qadhafi, in the
style of an Old Testament prophet, withdrew for
inspiration to the desert whence he had come. He
invariably came back bursting with energy.)

The climate of resentful hostility convinced
Shalhi's group that in spite of the ban on British

personnel, the government would secretly welcome Qadhafi's overthrow and do nothing serious to prevent it.

America was a more difficult problem. Shalhi's English associates knew their way round Whitehall but were less well placed to penetrate the inner thinking of the State Department, the Pentagon, the CIA and the powerful American oil companies. While America had not suffered the same humiliations as Britain, its interests had not been wholly spared. Like Britain, it had lost a base, the giant 100 million dollar Wheelus complex, and the predominantly American owned oil companies had been forced to disgorge revenue on an unprecedented scale. In two rounds of fierce negotiations, extending from February 1970 to April 1971, the young officers pushed up the price of Libyan oil by nearly a dollar and a quarter per barrel, from 2.21 dollars to 3.45. And this, it was becoming painfully clear, was only the beginning. How rough would Qadhafi have to be with the companies before he was marked out as an enemy of America? It was a question which Shalhi puzzled over a lot.

As befits a world power, the United States has an intelligence capability second to none, voracious for information on the men, events and situations affecting, even remotely, the interests of America. The CIA's knowledge of Libya was, and is, equalled only by Egypt's.

Two years before Qadhafi seized power, riots in the Tripoli docks triggered by the Six Day War and the subsequent arrest of a handful of political subversives alerted the CIA to the possibility that Libya might one day be taken over from within. The agency immediately had to direct its resources to answering such questions as: would the West's treaties with Idris be effective against a *coup d'état*? Did the bases have a long-term future? Who would take over from the aged Idris?

The CIA does this sort of operation thoroughly.

The Americans believe in blanket coverage, in the concept of 'total information.' It is a bad day for the CIA if, somewhere in the world, a coup happens which it has not forecast. Heads of station and their operatives on the spot can be sure of being hauled over the coals, if not posted elsewhere or fired outright.

In the months before Qadhafi's coup, the Americans had penetrated his God-fearing secret society, as they had no doubt equally penetrated rival groups of left-wing radicals—and, indeed, Shalhi's own circle of influential friends. In such a situation, the agency's brief is usually a watching one, to establish who is who rather than to help any one group to power.

When Qadhafi emerged on top the American government greeted the news with greater equanimity than the perhaps less well informed British. Two senior diplomatists helped swing American attitudes in favour of Qadhafi: David Newson and Joseph Palmer. Newson was ambassador in Tripoli, Palmer assistant secretary of state in Washington. Just before the coup they swapped jobs. And, on 4 September 1969, it was the well-briefed Newson whom the British ambassador to the United States, John Freeman, called on to discuss the matter of recognition.

Against the alarmists who saw the coup as a triumph for both Egypt and the Russians, extending Soviet influence into the western Mediterranean, Newson and Palmer argued that Qadhafi should be given a chance. In his despatches to Washington the wise, genial Bostonian, Joseph Palmer, prophesied that Qadhafi would prove to be a heaven-sent champion of American interests. Qadhafi was a committed Arab nationalist, an unquestioned revolutionary, a fervent progressive—but also as great a scourge of international communism as the late John Foster Dulles! It was urgent State Department intervention which restrained the black American brigadier general commanding Wheelus Field from obeying his instinct to march on Tripoli and restore the old regime.

Providentially for Palmer's thesis, a little incident occurred in Libya which went largely unnoticed in the world outside. In the early weeks of the revolution a translation into Arabic of a Soviet book critical of Islam appeared on the Tripoli market. Rumour has it that the book was circulated by the CIA. In any event it served the purpose of deeply offending Qadhafi and envenoming his relations with the Russians. The Soviet embassy was driven to issue a statement to the effect that the book had never been intended for export, but was for internal Soviet consumption only—an explanation which did nothing to help. Before the end of the year the United States consolidated its position by tipping off Qadhafi about a plot being hatched by Colonels Adnan Hawaz and Musa Ahmad, the newly appointed ministers of defence and the interior. The conspirators were arrested with twenty-three others, tried and jailed for life.

So much for Qadhafi's first year. The Americans felt things could have been a good deal worse. Granted, Qadhafi was a trifle half-baked perhaps, a bit of an Islamic hot-gospeller, somewhat neurotic about drink (although they noted that the oil companies were spared a rigorous interpretation of his ban on liquor); but at least he seemed honest, and anyway was vastly preferable to a rabid communist.

Qadhafi's second year as master of Libya, however, brought evidence of a change. The death of Nasser gave him a new importance in American eyes, one not altogether welcome. He was a thorn in Russian flesh all right, publicly scolding the Palestinian guerrillas of Marxist persuasion, helping President Sadat stand firm against Soviet pressure. But, with Nasser's restraint removed, he looked like becoming a dangerous activist. He was handing out cheques to trouble-makers all over the place, from black Muslims in the United States to Eritrean rebels against Emperor Haile Selassie of Ethiopia. He was also doing his best to fan the Arab-Israeli conflict into flame. He needed watching.

Shalhi and his associates had to weigh very carefully what would be the American reaction to their counter-coup. They judged that Qadhafi's aggressive oil policy, his general disruptiveness, his· threat to an eventual Palestine settlement would outweigh his emerging anticommunism in American eyes. He was a rash friend to have in these days of East-West detente. How much more comfortable life would be for the United States if Shalhi were in power in Tripoli! They had good reason to believe that America would let them get on with it.

13 The Price of Security

The breaking of Jeff Thompson's nerve sent a spasm of unease through the ranks of his associates. It raised the spectre they had hoped never to face that somewhere along the line their operation had been blown, penetrated—or betrayed.

Arriving hotfoot and shaken at the Naples headquarters on 29 January, Jeff was nevertheless persuaded to drive on to Trieste the next day to meet Conquistador XIII due from Bari on the 31st. Until he could be replaced on board, someone had to maintain communications with the ship. He spent the 31st, a Sunday, walking from the docks to the *stazione marittima* and back, smoking endless cigarettes and scanning the sea. No boat. His disquiet grew. With nerves on the stretch he returned at nightfall to his hotel just in time to take a telephone call. He recognised that crisp, unfriendly English voice. It was the SIS man from Bari proposing to call on him at eight o'clock next morning, and not troubling to be polite about it.

Jeff did not sleep much that night. He was up at dawn, packed his bag, paid his bill, and was on the road by seven, heading north for the Austrian

frontier. He noticed with a shudder that he was being
followed by two Italian police cars, but they kept
their distance. It looked as if their aim was less to
stop him than show him off the premises. Nearing the
border and uncertain of the road, Jeff stopped, and
'when the police pulled in behind him, walked back to
ask the way. 'Follow me,' invited one of the grinning
officers, and so, with police before and behind, Jeff
was courteously but firmly seen off Italian soil. Wild
horses would not have dragged him back.

He turned in his Hertz car at Munich, traced Kent
by telephone to Frankfurt and flew there himself that
night to say that as far as he was concerned this was
the end of the line.

The hotel at Frankfurt's sprawling new airport is a
comfortable and well-run establishment, but it is not
a friendly place in which to cope alone with a major
crisis. When Jeff Thompson departed for London,
Kent locked himself up for a day's hard thinking.

How was he to keep the operation together?
Shalhi, whom Kent saw briefly at Geneva airport on
his way to Frankfurt, had been surly on hearing of
the latest setback, but William was the one who took
it really badly. He who had always met adversity so
well was distraught at the defection of Jeff
Thompson. He seemed to think that without Jeff the
operation could not be attempted, and Kent had
great trouble making him understand that Jeff's
continued connection would, on the contrary,
guarantee Britain's actively stopping the strike. Once
again Kent wondered whether William really wanted
the assignment to succeed.

In Paris Léon was also showing signs of temperament. He had been forced to disperse his men and send them home only hours before they were due to catch their trains for Sicily. There had been a great many embarrassing phone calls to make, and lame excuses. By now he was very nervous about security. His friends in SDECE expressed a robust and cynical indifference to his Libyan escapade—there was little chance of its being attributed to them. But they did warn him to be careful as the Americans seemed to be taking a growing interest in the affair.

Everybody was looking to Kent for reassurance. Only he held all the separate strands of the operation, only he knew all the personalities involved. It was up to him to determine the facts, judge the dimensions of the security breakdown, and provide Shalhi with firm conclusions about what had gone wrong. These were the problems to which he had to turn his intelligence officer's mind in the Airport Hotel.

Security is something which has to be weighed economically. The only way to be sure of a hundred per cent security is to do nothing. But do nothing, and nothing happens. To get results, risks have to be taken and some compromise made with the ideal of total security. The planners of every secret operation have to decide for themselves the extent of the compromise they can afford, the economic break-even point. In each case the level of security adopted should be a matter of deliberate decision.

From the start Kent was aware that the Hilton assignment could not fully protect itself against the intelligence agencies of the major powers. The Libyans presented no great problem, but he had no

illusions that he and his associates could take on a
sophisticated service: they had neither the resources
nor the discipline. The British and American secret
services had been alerted to the operation from the
first. At any stage they, or the French or the Italians,
could stop them in ways which gave no redress—
Conquistador could, for instance, be' rammed
'accidentally' at sea; individuals could be held on
trumped up charges for long enough to sabotage the
operation. It would not need much inventiveness if
they really wanted to spike the assignment.

What Kent was counting on was great power
indifference or, better still, tacit connivance. His real
enemy was the press. It would need only a paragraph
in a newspaper to blow the operation and Shalhi's
hopes sky-high.

Until the harassment of Jeff in Italy it looked as if
Kent had been operating on the right economic level
of security. Not one journalist in the dozen or so
countries connected with the assignment had picked
up so much as a whisper. There had been countless
opportunities for the great powers to intervene, but
they had not done so. What had now gone wrong? Had
some new factor arisen, forcing him to reappraise the
whole security issue? At Bari and Trieste both the
Italian police and the British secret service had shown
their hand, and it had not been a helping hand. Were
the British and Italians working together, and to what
end?

Thinking systematically through the operation,
step by step, Kent discarded the possibility that the
British had kept up with him at every move. To
devote such resources of surveillance just would not

have been worth their while. The most plausible
explanation was that Italian coastguards had spotted
Conquistador XIII at Bari, perhaps even earlier, at
Brindisi or in the Straits of Messina, and had thought
her worth a second look because of her functional
outline. If she and her passengers had looked more
ordinary, if this had not been Mafia territory, the
matter might have been dismissed after the police
search of the boat revealed nothing. But with the
large, tough-looking crew on board, lingering several
days at Bari, the authorities must have decided on a
further check.

Jeff's presence might then have set them
wondering what an Englishman was up to in such
company. The Italian police would have flashed his
name to the British police who, through Special
Branch, might have asked the security service for a
trace, and very soon Jeff's SAS past and his
connection with Watchguard could have emerged. In
view of the veto conveyed to Stirling the secret
service would start to ask what Jeff Thompson was
doing at Bari and whether another British team was
lying somewhere off shore ready to go. What the
British would not have known was that Jeff was
merely acting as ship's agent, and that no Englishman
was going on a fighting mission to Tripoli. Obviously
they were still worried about British involvement.

Kent determined to find out whether this was so.
His hypothesis seemed confirmed when, on arriving in
London on 8 February, he learned that the British
authorities had been checking with John Brooke
Miller—and even with David Stirling. Coming home
from abroad earlier that month Miller had been

stopped by a passport officer at Heathrow, then handed a message by a security official. It was to telephone his SIS contact who, when Miller obliged, accused him of disobeying the veto and intending to go in with the assault. Nothing could have been further from the truth.

Bigger guns were used on Stirling. He was invited to call on first a senior Foreign Office official and then the Foreign Secretary, Sir Alec Douglas-Home. Sir Alec and Colonel Stirling were old acquaintances, and while Sir Alec was in opposition from 1964 to the Conservative victory in June 1970, Stirling would sometimes drop in to see him at his London flat to talk over the international situation. This time he could tell Sir Alec little except that he himself had withdrawn in 1970. He believed that James Kent had remained in contact with Umar al-Shalhi, but as far as he knew British personnel were no longer involved in the planned operation.

The odd thing was that the SIS had harried Jeff, reproached Miller and urged Stirling to use his influence, but they had not approached the man best equipped to give the answers. James Kent decided that if they were curious about what was happening, they had better come and talk to him. He asked a friend to pass on his telephone number to the right quarters (not that they did not know it already), as an indication of his willingness to hear what they had to say. Within twenty-four hours an appointment had been made at Kent's club—for meetings of such importance he considered it desirable to have the initiative of when and where.

Not to volunteer information was one of Kent's

principles; to admit nothing unnecessarily was another, although in this encounter his discretion could be little more than a fig-leaf. The authorities knew he was involved with Shalhi, and Kent knew they knew; but secret services like to cap ninety-nine per cent knowledge with the certainty of an admission. This they were denied. Kent did not admit to being Shalhi's collaborator and talked throughout in hypothetical terms.

The verbal sparring took place over two meetings. Predictably Kent argued that to bring Qadhafi down was in British interests, all the more so if it were done by foreign mercenaries, while the British official was equally convinced that failure would result in Britain's being the first target of Qadhafi's wrath. The Libyan leader was dotty enough to strike out in revenge at anybody and everybody.

There was no reconciling such opposed views. The official tried another tack. 'Well,' he said, 'if you're so sure it's a good thing to do, and if you have the right assets—armed men ready to go in, political support at the other end, perhaps other things we don't know about—why don't we talk it over? You tell me all about it, and perhaps we can help after all.'

Not on your life! This was Kent's reaction to the siren-song, but he kept it to himself. To tell all would be the first step towards being taken over, towards the operation's being diverted from its purpose and generally frustrated for other people's reasons. He guessed the British wanted to know everything. He felt certain they could do nothing. He turned down the invitation.

One of the themes which emerged in the

conversations was British dislike for Shalhi. Kent was told that, even if a coup were to be considered, Shalhi, known to be unscrupulous, perhaps unstable and corrupt, was not the right man to lead it. Surely he was insufficiently acceptable to the Libyan people. Kent pointed out that Shalhi's coup was to be made in the name of King Idris and that he did not intend to accept formal power himself. Anyway Kent could not accept the British estimate of the Arab's character. He had seen a side of Shalhi which the British did not know about, his steadiness of purpose, his coolness in adversity. It was easy to write off the Shalhi family as unsuitable, but who were the alternatives? Both Kent and the Foreign Office knew the Libyan opposition batting order, and in it Shalhi was opening batsman, followed by nothing but a lot of rabbits.

Kent could not pretend that he had won over his adversary—quite the contrary: the official attitude to the Hilton assignment was evidently hardening. At the start, back in May 1970, it had seemed to favour Qadhafi's overthrow. By August this had cooled to a ban on the use of British personnel. Now the view seemed to be 'We don't much like it, whichever way it's played.' Was there behind this increasing hostility some further pressure which Kent did not know of? Perhaps the British merely felt that the build-up had gone on too long, and they could close their eyes no longer.

But if they had really wanted to sabotage Shalhi's plans, they could simply have told Kent that the Libyans knew all about the operation and would be waiting for Conquistador. This the British had never even hinted at. Was there a crumb of encouragement here?

Italy was a separate threat. In calculating the security risks Kent had to consider that the Italian police might have acted against Jeff at Britain's request. He believed the coincidence of the SIS man's appearance and the searching of Conquistador by the Italians to be the fruit of Anglo-Italian liaison on police and security matters.

But the speed and thoroughness of the Italian swoop suggested another explanation: that behind the events at Bari and Trieste lay a high-level Italian government decision. Under this second hypothesis the Italians had good reasons of their own for interfering.

Shalhi had many acquaintances in Italian public life, in particular one contact with influence in the presidency, and when he learned that the plan involved his and William's boarding Conquistador at an Italian port, he resolved to pull a few strings to ensure a safe embarkation. He approached his contact and cautiously inquired what the authorities' reaction would be to a shipment of arms for the tribes in Cyrenaica being secretly moved into Libya through an Italian port. Could they be induced to overlook it? A senior Italian official subsequently saw Shalhi in a German city, and the suggestion was made that Shalhi personally should take the matter further at a higher level in Rome.

This approach may have done Shalhi no good and could even have done him harm. His move very likely prodded the *Servizio Informazioni Difesa*(SID),

Italy's intelligence and security service, into investigating his affairs. A report on his proposed Cyrenaican arms operation was probably passed by SID to the Reserved Affairs Office of the Ministry of the Interior, which in turn may have alerted the political squads of the Public Security Forces—the equivalent of the British Special Branch, organised in Italy on a provincial basis—to keep an eye open for suspicious looking vessels. Only some such procedure could adequately explain the lively and sustained interest shown in Conquistador by the authorities at Bari, whether they connected the boat with Shalhi or not.

In asking for help, Shalhi may have misread Italian political attitudes towards Qadhafi, and counted too straight-forwardly on˙ their being resentful. He assumed that Qadhafi's unceremonious expulsion of over thirty thousand Italians had aroused such enmity that the Italians would be only too happy to see someone snub the Libyan colonel. The Italian mission sent to Tripoli to discuss the affairs of the dispossessed settlers had been rudely treated. It had not been allowed to question the expulsions and sequestrations, but only to make suggestions about the administration of these measures. They had come back very much abashed.

Shalhi's assumptions were correct insofar as the extreme right wing in Italy was concerned. It loathed, and continues to loathe, Qadhafi, and would take any opportunity to revenge the settlers. For example, it was undoubtedly extreme right wing sympathisers in the Ministry of Defence in Rome who, in August 1972, leaked news of the shipment to Qadhafi's government of Italian arms—in the hope of putting an end to such deals. Neither is there much love lost for Qadhafi personally, or indeed for the Arabs in general, in the intelligence and security apparatus of the three Italian armed services, known as SIOS (*Servizi Informazioni Operazioni Segrete*). It is probably fair to say that both SID and SIOS prefer the more efficient Israelis to the troublesome Arabs.

But the key to understanding how things really work in Italy lies elsewhere. The general direction of policy is not determined by the secret service, military intelligence or the extreme right. Nor for that matter is it wholly determined by the cabinet or even the prime minister. Effective power lies with two groups of men, rivals bound inextricably together by the system. They are the bosses of the various factions inside the Christian Democratic Party on the one hand and, on the other, the heads of financial-industrial groups in the public sector, corporations created or controlled by the Christian Democrats and which in turn influence them. Whoever nominally heads the Italian government, more important in the making of policy are such Christian Democratic bosses as Amintore Fanfani, Aldo Moro and Giulio Andreotti, and the managers of the powerful state-owned international oil corporation ENI.

What Shalhi may not have realised was that these influential men favour a 'Mediterranean policy' for Italy, aimed at giving their country more weight in the Mediterranean area. The Christian Democrat-controlled ENI is the chosen instrument in this search for influence. The word handed down from the real centres of power in Italy is that anything likely to offend the Arabs is to be avoided wherever possible. In particular, friendship with Qadhafi, so close across the sea, must be maintained whatever the hardships suffered by a few thousand luckless settlers. (This policy paid off in September 1972 with the signing of a concession agreement with Libya which gave ENI an estimated twelve million tons of oil a year.)

Such considerations explain why the Italian police cracked down on Libyan exiles in Rome; why they tolerated the presence in their cities of suspected Palestinian terrorists such as the Libyan-financed Wail Zuaitar (believed to be connected with Black September and assassinated in Rome on 16 October 1972); and why, at the important level of Italian policy making, Shalhi's activities, even if thought unlikely to be effective, were certain to be viewed with extreme disfavour as likely to upset a carefully planned apple-cart.

In Italy there were plenty of people in high places with pro-Arab leanings, but none of this sentiment could benefit Shalhi.

Faced with clear evidence of hostile surveillance by both British and Italian agents, Kent's immediate task was to readjust the economic level of security. He felt sure that the Italians, and possibly the British as well, were tapping telephones to try and piece together what was happening. In any country telephone tapping is a lengthy and tedious business, involving the recording, transcription and examination of tapes. If the investigators are not to be swamped in a mass of irrelevant material, tapping can be attempted only selectively, for limited periods and on very important cases. Where criminal cases are concerned, there is the quite different problem of how to make public use of the material, perhaps in court, without betraying the source. Policemen often have to go to great lengths to pretend the information was secured by other means. So telephone tapping is a clumsy instrument, but it can be effective. It was a threat which Kent could not afford to ignore.

In Italy he cut telephone communication to the absolute minimum. In Britain, where tapping is scrupulously controlled, requiring in each case a warrant signed by the Home Secretary, Kent still felt uneasy enough to take evasive action. At this critical point in the operation he moved on his visits to London into the Grosvenor House Hotel or Claridge's, and booked as well a room at the Hilton on nights when he had sensitive calls to make. They were expensive phone calls, but the advantage of the Hilton was that he could dial out himself, without the help of the hotel switchboard.

Shalhi too redoubled his precautions. He had always been careful, always assuming that he was at risk, but now with Kent he took great pains to keep their contacts clandestine, in order to prevent their meetings being bugged or even noticed. At Bari the surveillance of Jeff and the crew had been clumsy and amateurish, perhaps deliberately so, but the principals had now to suppose that they would be the target of more sophisticated operations. Constant, unscheduled movement seemed to offer the only protection. Frankfurt, Hamburg, Vienna, Munich . . .. Never did they meet twice running in the same place.

All the arrangements had to be reviewed. Italy was too hot a country from which to embark a team undetected. Kent would have to devise a new plan to get the principals and the men on board Conquistador free from all interference. The options were diminishing. More than ever the operation would have to be mounted in space.

Fortunately for Shalhi, Kent was not a man to be easily dismayed. Implicit in his philosophy of private initiatives was the confidence to brave official displeasure and chart his own course. He was not torn by doubt. With a clear conscience he judged that Shalhi's assignment was not against British interests. Officialdom disagreed, but officials had no monopoly of wisdom, and he would go on undeterred. He did not think he was blinded by his will to succeed, or that his judgment was impaired. On the contrary, with information flooding in to stretch his powers to the limit, he saw the whole complex machine he had constructed with the brilliant clarity that danger gives. Here was a situation where words, thoughts, speculation were not enough. The only real way to test the resolve of his enemies, the attitude of the British, the Italian, or indeed of any other government was to go ahead, dare them physically to stop him, call their bluff. After six months of nerve-testing, he was totally committed to the storming of the Hilton and would see it through or bust.

14 Thumbs Down
in Rome

A more prudent man than Shalhi would have given up. But the time for prudence had passed. In a hard fought contest the prize falls to the one who at the final moment throws in a last reserve of strength and courage. He may destroy himself in the attempt, but there comes a time when caution has to be forgotten, restraint abandoned, and the outcome staked on a fearless throw. It was in such a do or die mood that Shalhi with William met James Kent at Hamburg on 19 February 1971.

They knew their backs were to the wall. There was the backwash of successive delays, the dwindling operational options, the looming security problems. But all three were gnawed by the frustration that they had so far been defeated by the perversity of circumstance and outside interference rather than by enemy action by the Libyans. One way and another a lot of money had been spent or committed—upwards of 600,000 dollars, a sobering figure for any bank balance. Quite apart from what they had been through together, the sheer size of this investment bound them to each other and drove them to a last attempt to get their money's worth. But there could be no more banter, no more reassurances. Without illusion about their chances, fully aware that the outlook was grim, the three men agreed to go on.

William was the most troubled. By nature he was a businessman, not a cafe politician: nor was he used to undercover intrigue. His had been the greatest personal sacrifice, seeing that he was separated from his wife and family, had lost his means of livelihood and had spent his savings. Now only Shalhi's presence kept·him from going to pieces. Shalhi himself seemed as composed as ever, less because he was better cushioned against adversity then because he had nerve and was a fatalist. If he was afraid, it was only that he would fail in what he conceived to be his duty. Kent was sustained by professional pride and determination not to be outsmarted.

All faced the dreaded possibility that to curry favour with the ever richer and more powerful Qadhafi, one or other of the major intelligence services involved would betray them to the Libyans. The Egyptians would certainly do so if they had a chance: they had penetrated at least the outer edges of Italian security—the political squads of the police, rather than SID or SIOS—and could well have picked up a scent of the affair. The Italians themselves might do it, to play a trump card in Tripoli. And where in the last analysis would the all-powerful CIA decide its interests lay?

In planning the strike it had been recognised from the start that the moment of maximum danger for the operation was when the three components—the men, the boat and the arms—were brought together. If the boat were searched at this point it would look bad indeed. So the plan had always been to put the team and principals aboard as late as possible, first at Bari and in the second attempt even further south, at Catania. But where could they now be embarked? Italy was out, and so, for reasons which had been thoroughly explored, were the French Mediterranean ports, Spain, Malta, the Greek islands. There was no harbour within Conquistador's range of Tripoli where twenty-five mercenaries could safely put to sea on a floating arsenal.

The logic of the problem drove Kent and Shalhi to decide in favour of a rendezvous at sea, in international waters south of Sicily.

Technically this was not difficult. With wireless communication it is not hard for two ships to rendezvous in mid-ocean or, in fair weather, for men to be transferred from one vessel to another. But it introduced fresh complexities, and the overall plan had to be reshaped accordingly.

A basic decision to be taken was whether Conquistador XIII was too blown to be used again. To replace her would take time, maybe several months, not to mention the cost involved. In spite of these drawbacks, Kent and William thought Conquistador should be replaced, but the decision was for Shalhi to make, and anxious to avoid a further long delay he chose to battle on with her. It was reckoned that, with no mercenaries or compromising gear on board, she had a fair chance of reaching Ploče without attracting unwelcome attention. She could then pick up the arms and explosives and head legally for the open sea, without running the gauntlet of Italian customs or the vigilant political squads.

Now for the other half of the equation: to get the men on board Conquistador in the middle of the Mediterranean, a second vessel had to be acquired. She would have to collect her passengers from a port uncontaminated by the ramifications of the Hilton assignment. Kent chose Morocco. He chartered a boat on wet lease at Casablanca, on the Atlantic coast, and arranged for her to sail to the Straits of Gibraltar. There Léon's team would be picked up at Tangier, and the Arab principals off Algeciras on the Spanish side of the Straits. Shalhi and William had no visas for Morocco and were reluctant at this stage to risk applying for them.

The rendezvous at sea cut down the time that the men would be on board with the weapons. This was a gain in security but it raised the new problem of broaching the arms crates, and degreasing, examining and testing the weapons and equipment in the short time before the assault—and all in a busy stretch of water regularly patrolled by the Russian navy and the Sixth Fleet, not to mention British and French warships and even the odd Egyptian patrol boat. It was estimated that the programme could just be fitted in.

But there was nothing but trouble in putting this plan into execution. For one thing Conquistador disappeared on its journey from Bari to Trieste, and was five long days out of contact, giving ground for the most agonised speculations that she had been rammed, sunk, or taken into custody on the high seas. In the event, she had merely had to heave to in dense fog off Ancona. To wipe the slate as clean as possible, Kent decided on a complete change of crew.

When Conquistador finally arrived at Trieste, she was met by a resourceful Glaswegian seaman called Jock Fraser whom Kent had sent down to take over Jeff's role as ship's agent. The four mercenaries who had joined the boat at Toulon were put on a train for Paris, the captain and crew were paid off and new men, recruited through Léon, came aboard. Fraser reported daily to Kent in brief, terse calls from out of the way phone boxes. Having been warned that the lines were monitored, he said little more than that he was alive and well. But for Kent it was good to know all the same.

Conquistador was a coastal craft, capable of speed but not endurance. She did not have the range to sail from Ploče to Tripoli and back to the safety of European waters without refuelling. At some cost twenty flexible fuel tanks were put on board, doubling her range. Everything seemed in order when, with only days to go, the ship's radar failed. In frantic haste Kent had to arrange for new equipment to be flown out from London, together with an expert to fit it. This snag cost another 3,000 dollars.

One anxiety creates another anxiety. All these delays raised doubts whether the consignment of explosives crated at Ploče was still in tip-top condition. The whole assault depended on the walls of the jail being breached within minutes. There would be no time for fumbling with damp fuses, no time to mould and wire up replacement charges. And so, to mop up this small but contagious area of misgiving, Kent sent the French explosives expert, posing as the representative of the Chad arms dealer, to Yugoslavia to open the explosives boxes and check that all was well. He returned satisfied.

But in general the mood of the French mercenaries was not one of satisfaction. The postponements deflated their enthusiasm, and some of the men indicated that they were pulling out altogether, dropping the assignment—which for a mercenary carries no shame or censure, being regarded not as desertion but merely a way of breaking a contract. The drop-outs were replaced and Kent had once again to make the necessary changes to the bank certified cheques in the Geneva safe deposit.

Léon was hard put to keep his team together, all the more so because he was jumpy himself. He had been more shaken than he cared to admit by Jeff Thompson's defection, partly because he had hoped all along that the solid Englishmen would come with them to Tripoli, but also because this unlikely couple, with little more than a phrase or two in a common language, had become close friends. Léon now found it difficult to explain Jeff's absence to the rest of the team without spreading further dismay.

As the odds lengthened against success Léon had to live with the possibility of death or injury to himself and his team on an assignment whose contours were to him still vague. He developed a weak stomach, and was reduced to pecking at bland dishes like steamed fish, washed down with a little white wine or Evian water. One evening to cheer him up Kent invited him to dinner at a celebrated Parisian sea-food restaurant, but poor Léon could only manage a few oysters.

He was satisfied that the Libyans had not penetrated Kent's organisation: the best guarantee in his eyes was Kent's willingness to go on. But he knew enough about what had happened in Italy and London to realise that the Hilton assignment had few secrets from the major Western intelligence services. It had also crossed his mind that one of these could tip off Qadhafi.

His SDECE contacts continued to warn him that the American attitude was now frankly hostile, and he was not sure whether the Americans could be trusted. But Kent, to whom he put these fears, tended to play them down, arguing that the British were much more of a threat. The Americans were unlikely to care very much seeing that this was basically a Libyan émigré initiative involving no American personnel.

On the eve of the strike James Kent set up his operational headquarters at the Airport Hotel at Frankfurt, while Shalhi and William established themselves in the town, at the Intercontinental. Kent instructed Léon to start moving his team south from the night of Friday, 19 March. Some of the men flew to Casablanca and travelled by road to Tangier, others went by train through France and Spain, crossing by ferry to the Moroccan coast. They were to sail on the charter vessel on Monday the 22nd, in order to reach the rendezvous at sea with Conquistador by the 28th. The assault on the Hilton was timed for the last night of March. The principals would fly to southern Spain on the morning of the 22nd to board the vessel off Algeciras.

With these arrangements in hand Kent turned his attention to Trieste, where Conquistador XIII, refuelled, revictualled and shipshape, was ready to sail

Conquistador XIII under police custody at Trieste, (Giornalfoto, Trieste).

for Ploče on Sunday, the 21st. In the late afternoon, to assure himself that the ship had weighed anchor as planned, Kent tried to reach Jock Fraser at his Trieste hotel. He could make little of the volubility of the hotel reception clerk, but the general drift seemed to be that the Scotsman was not around. As the evening wore on Kent telephoned again and again, but Fraser was still missing.

The explanation, when Kent learned it the next morning, was stark and simple. The boat had been seized and his man was in prison.

Conquistador was doomed before she made a move. Unknown to Kent or Shalhi, a high-level decision had been made in Rome to stop her putting to sea. In the meantime her radio was to be monitored and every movement of her crew shadowed. These instructions were sent to the political squad of the Trieste carabinieri who, in co-operation with the harbour master, set up a twenty-four hour command post in the port area, and deployed a considerable force of security agents. Rome indicated to the local police that this was no petty case of smuggling, but a political affair of international importance.

When at twelve noon on Sunday, 21 March 1971, the captain gave the order to cast off, armed men came pouring on to the quay from the harbour sheds and boarded the boat. Conquistador was sequestered and searched, the crew interrogated, the captain taken into custody. Jock Fraser was arrested at his hotel and held incommunicado.

It was not until the next morning that Kent, having failed to reach Fraser, contacted the Trieste shipping agency which had acted for him in clearing the new radar through customs. Very stiffly the manager announced what had happened, giving Kent the name of the agency's lawyer. Kent telephoned him, asked him to take on the case, and cabled off a five hundred dollar advance on his fee.

He had one or two other gloomy tasks to perform: to recall Léon and his men from Tangier, dismiss the charter vessel, and, worse still, halt the principals, then on the point of leaving their Frankfurt hotel to fly to southern Spain.

After that there was nothing to do but drown their sorrows. Men without a country, Shalhi and William came up to Kent's suite at the Airport Hotel at 9.30 on the morning of Tuesday 23 March. They had all striven hard, but had been defeated by overwhelming odds. There were no recriminations. All day they sat there drinking champagne and eating nothing, talking disconnectedly of this and that, as people do when suddenly stripped of tension and purpose. Shalhi spoke of his youth at court, told stories of the gentle Idris, the millionaire philanthropist with holes in his slippers. They drank, kept up their courage, reassured each other—but refused to cry.

15 The Protectors

Who was protecting Qadhafi, and why?

Without knowing it, the young ruler of Libya was saved—at least for the moment—from internal upheaval if not from death. The blow aimed against him from across the Mediterranean was parried as if by divine intervention. Sitting in his bare office in the Tripoli barracks, he was guarded by invisible lines of defence which had nothing to do with his Free Officers, his little army, his General Investigation Directorate, his new squadrons of Mirage aircraft, or any other proud trappings of revolutionary nationhood.

Who wanted Qadhafi to survive? The overt evidence suggests that Britain and Italy, whether alone or in liaison, shielded him. With surgical precision they stalled the Hilton assignment at the moment of take off. But this is not the whole story.

The events at Bari and Trieste of January-March 1971 were only the tip of a powerful iceberg whose hidden ramifications reach far into the workings of international politics. A lone assassin who swiftly and suddenly puts a bullet in his victim outflanks forces he cannot hope to take on. But Shalhi's operation, relatively small-scale though it was, needed numbers and preparation and stretched across many countries. Because of the initial setback—the failure of the boat and the arms to turn up at Bari in November 1970—and because of the subsequent delays, it set up ripples which reached the sensitive detectors of the major Western secret services, thus bringing wider interests into play. The powers had to take stock of what Umar al-Shalhi and James Kent were up to, and judge how it affected what they themselves were up to. And they found there was a conflict. Inevitably the machinery of surveillance and prevention outstripped the ingenuity and limited resources of the planners of the assault.

The thwarting of Shalhi was many-layered, and to understand how it was done successive skins have to be peeled from the onion. It can validly be argued that the Italians seized Conquistador because ENI and the Christian Democratic Party bosses did not want anyone to upset their Mediterranean policy of friendship with Qadhafi. Less convincingly, the British may have driven Jeff Thompson off the scene because they feared a backlash against their already threatened Libyan interests.

But there is strong reason to believe that both British and Italians were prompted to take action by a still greater power, the United States of America, and that it was this prompting which in the last analysis tipped the scale. For reasons of its own, which accorded with Italy's but perhaps conflicted with Britain's, America had a stake in the health and safety of Qadhafi.

Police forces of the world work closely together

whenever necessary. Even countries which dislike and distrust each other will pool their efforts against a criminal, in an organisation such as Interpol, for instance. But liaison between secret services is both more complex and more significant. It is the acid test of the links between two countries, of the degree of trust, the relative strength, the interdependence. Just as relations between countries are rarely equal, so are relations between secret services. Liaison means, in effect, who controls whom.

Some intelligence services are unbeatable on their own ground. West Germany's Gehlen organisation, for example, was excellent at containing East Germany and uncovering Communist intentions—at least until the thaw of Willy Brandt's *Ostpolitik*. Similarly no one knows more about the intrigues of Iranian students abroad than the Shah's dreaded security service Savak. Egyptian intelligence ably penetrates Egypt's sister Arab states. Britain, who once had a service fit for an empire, has recently switched its Foreign Office effort from Asia and Africa to Europe where its destiny now lies, and doubtless to good effect.

But for global knowledge, global power is needed, and vice versa. Only two intelligence services have the resources and the interests to operate world wide—the Russian *Komitet Gosudarstvennoy Bezopasnosti* (KGB) and the American CIA. In the geographical arena of the Hilton assignment—Europe, the Mediterranean and North Africa—the CIA is unchallengeably cock of the roost. Its business is to know everything.

In the search for total knowledge, the CIA

establishes close liaison where it can, and particularly with America's NATO partners. It is a reasonable assumption that in the CIA's co-operation with Italy's SID, for example, the flow of information is heavier one way than the other. America will get more than it gives: and justifiably. While the Italian government has no pressing need for minute data on internal American politics, America must keep itself informed about the country with the largest Communist party outside the Soviet block. What liaison does not yield, penetration may. Whatever the channel, Washington could undoubtedly warn Rome that Conquistador XIII was engaged in a serious political operation and press for preventative action.

In spite of its image of unprincipled blundering, the heritage of its youth, the CIA has, as far as can be judged, become an extremely effective instrument in the last decade. Its connection with Britain's SIS has moved a long way from the 1940s when American intelligence came to school in England. The pupil has long since outstripped the teacher, deploying not only far greater resources but also a political will to action which Britain has lost.

Nowadays Britain is beyond dispute the junior partner and in its handling of the Hilton assignment appears to have behaved as such. From the moment of Qadhafi's emergence Britain and America consulted each other regularly about him, and there is reason to suppose that it was American pressure which caused Whitehall's attitude to veer from scarcely veiled hostility towards the Libyan to a clandestine intervention to protect him—in spite of the threat he represented to British interests. The

British must have been told that the United States would not tolerate an attack on Qadhafi, thus forcing them, even reluctantly, to warn off first Colonel Stirling, then Jeff Thompson, eventually Kent. In 1970-71 Britain was in poor shape for taking independent international action. The Commonwealth had collapsed as an effective institution and Europe had still not opened its doors. At this crucial moment, Whitehall was not much interested in anything happening beyond the frontiers of the Common Market.

Would the French have been so amenable to an American directive? Even though French mercenaries were to storm the Hilton from a French-manned boat refitted in a French boatyard, the SDECE displayed throughout a cool lack of concern. They certainly knew what was afoot, from Léon if from no other source. But they never intervened.

Yet on the face of it France's interest in North Africa was at least as great as Italy's. Linked historically to Algeria, Morocco and Tunisia, France too has a 'Mediterranean policy,' and in Libya the Mirage deal spearheaded the way for big trade and diplomatic rewards. In the opinion of French diplomatists, the new regime in Libya is doing an admirable job and when Qadhafi sent Jallud to Paris, the young major had the red carpet of the Elysée Palace unrolled for him. How do these facts square with French official indifference to Shalhi's activities?

These are two good reasons why the French authorities chose to ignore the Hilton assignment. One was that the trade bonus won in Libya was too recent and unexpected for the defence of Qadhafi to have become an intelligence priority. A more cogent reason was that SDECE could not take a firm line on this little intrigue being deep in internal conflict marked by purges and counter-purges, the legacy of two troubled decades of French history.

During his presidency General de Gaulle had packed the secret service with his own men and ordered it first to crush the Algerian settlers' OAS and then, as the General's feud with America developed in the 1960s, to treat the CIA as a hostile service. As a result SDECE was riven by pro- and anti-gaullist factions, by defenders of the American connection and opponents of it, by fellow-travellers and extreme rightists. When the Hilton assignment was hatched in the second half of 1970, General de Gaulle had gone, Pompidou was president and SDECE had a new boss, Alexandre de Marenches, whose unenviable task was to clean the service up, restructure it and bring it back into the Western camp. At the same time the American and French police forces began to co-operate closely in hounding down international drug traffickers.

By the early spring of 1971, SDECE was itself close enough to the CIA for its men to learn of American hostility to Shalhi and convey as much to Léon. But with its own problems to solve, it steered clear of the anti-Qadhafi operation, probably on the cynical principle that it could safely leave the sabotage to the Americans, keeping its own hands clean.

From the moment the Americans learned of Shalhi's plan—perhaps as early as Reynolds's meeting with the Libyan exiles in Rome in May 1970—they

would not have left it alone. As top service in the
international pecking order, the CIA could not risk
ignorance. It would have the benefit of information
flowing from its liaison with SID, SDECE and the
SIS, from its contact with Colonel Stirling, and very
likely from Yassin Ubaid, the engineer of the
counterplot. At the same time it would be watching
the situation on the ground in Libya.

But at this level, that of the physical defence of
Qadhafi and his regime, the main responsibility would
fall less on the CIA than on Egyptian intelligence.
Whereas America can supply external protection,
Egypt provides within Libya itself the first line of
defence, thus representing another skin of the onion
of Qadhafi's safety.

If the Americans, the British, the Italians and the
French had all allowed the Hilton assignment to take
off Egypt might well have tried to crush it on Libyan
soil. Egypt's need for union with Libya has already
furnished Qadhafi with two battalions, a squadron of
jets, and an excellent intelligence network—and in
addition, no doubt, a counter-coup capability of
some sophistication; for, like the CIA, Egypt's service
is not content passively to collect intelligence, but is
geared to turning it into action.

It would be a formidable task for any assailant to
penetrate the double defence lines of Egypt and
America. Qadhafi is, at the time of writing, more
secure than perhaps he knows himself.

Why should the mighty United States, Israel's firmest
friend, take such pains to protect Israel's most
implacable enemy? Among the rulers of the Arab

world none is so committed as Qadhafi to the recovery of Palestine from the Jews. And yet America pulled many secret strings to make sure that the Hilton assignment failed. What was the thinking that lay behind these moves?

For one thing Qadhafi's growing importance since the death of Nasser attracted America's attention as it attracted the world's. Here was a ruler who had not only money in very large quantities, but also other assets. His ideology was a winning package of nostalgia for Arab glory, hopes for Arab reconquest and a back-to-the-Koran fundamentalism, a package with immense grass-roots appeal to the whole Arab world. Qadhafi also had will power and a flair for flamboyant action. He practised what he preached. With all these advantages the young Libyan was cast for international stardom.

It is an instinct of great powers, when confronted with phenomena like Qadhafi, to attempt to make them into friends. Qadhafi met the Americans more than half way. Since the early days of the coup, when the American ambassador Joseph Palmer passed word of his anti-communism to Washington, Qadhafi did nothing to dispel this view. In fact his hatred for godless Marxism grew daily more ferocious, and he set himself on a course to root out and destroy every trace of Soviet influence in the Middle East.

He helped thwart the Communist takeover of the Sudan; he encouraged President Sadat of Egypt to expel his Russian advisers; he waged, and continues to wage, a war of attrition against Arab Marxists in Baghdad, Aden and Damascus. He is well on the way to robbing the Russians of the political fruits of fifteen years of heavy investment and hard work in the area. If he did not exist perhaps the Americans would have invented him.

American policy was to let him get on with the good work, to protect him discreetly against his enemies, and not to cramp his style by backing him too publicly.

Qadhafi is, therefore, a valuable element in America's power game, but the truth is that quite apart from his contribution, America has from about 1970 onwards never had it so good in the Middle East. It is the dominant power. Britain, a friend but also a rival, has effectively withdrawn from the area, while the Soviet Union, whose influence soared so alarmingly after 1955, has seen its popularity slump since the Arab defeat of 1967.

By destroying Nasser's power in the June War Israel demonstrated the limits of Russian friendship: Russia was not going to risk a confrontation with America on behalf of the Arabs—as was made even plainer during the Nixon-Brezhnev summit in Moscow in the summer of 1972. At that meeting the two super-powers agreed to contain the Arab-Israeli conflict in the Middle East and not allow it to endanger their global East-West thaw. This amounted to Russia's acquiescing to the Arabs remaining the underdogs, and conceding the primacy of America and its Israeli protégé in the area.

To consolidate this advantage and secure its future access to oil supplies, America has been busily stitching together a conservative defence line across the Middle East, in which the main strong points are the great oil producing countries of Iran, Saudi

Arabia—and Libya. In the building of this front, Qadhafi has played a role useful to America in mopping up Communist positions and, even more importantly, in wooing Arab minds from the seductions of Marxism-Leninism. Before his emergence 'scientific socialism' was all the vogue, among intellectuals everywhere, Palestinian guerrillas, and even to some extent the Arab masses. But Qadhafi is both product and cause of a traditionalist and Islamic backlash now sweeping all before it.

From America's point of view this favourable picture is spoiled by two ugly blots. The first is the still running sore of Arab-Israeli fear and hatred, spilling its poison into Arab relations with the West and constantly threatening to erupt into violence. The other is the disastrous plight of the Egyptians, the great unlucky have-nots in the random shareout of Arab wealth, who yet bear the brunt of the confrontation with Israel and as a result are ground down into social chaos.

Both problems constitute a latent threat to America's long-term Middle East interests, and there is no doubt that President Nixon would like to be the architect of an overall settlement. Both problems are however linked—and a potential key to their solution lies in Libya, another reason for American concern for Qadhafi.

At its simplest the Israeli-Egyptian quarrel, currently the knottiest problem in the larger Arab-Israeli quarrel, is about territory. Israel wants to keep a substantial slice of the Sinai Peninsula captured from Egypt in 1967, and in particular Sharm al-Shaikh dominating the head of the Red Sea. Egypt wants to recover the whole of Sinai as a precondition of peace. How to break the stalemate? Israel is the stronger and therefore immovable. In American eyes the problem is to devise a formula which will make it possible for Egypt to concede.

The idea to which American policy has apparently been edging is to compensate Egypt for its lost territory in Sinai in the east by helping her swallow Libya in the west. America did not initiate the Egyptian-Libyan union, but once the project was announced began to see it not only as a lifeline for crowded, .poverty-stricken Egypt, but also as providing a possible breakthrough to the long sought Arab-Israeli peace.

Of all his countrymen, only Qadhafi has the will, stature and commitment to Arab unity to deliver over his country to Egypt. So, agreed on little else, America and Egypt for their different reasons are agreed on the need to keep Colonel Qadhafi in power, at least for the time being.

In spite of his messianic fervour, Qadhafi is a realist with an instinct for the workings of power. He probably knows that so long as he suits America's global policies, and so long as he plays ball with Egypt, the CIA and Egyptian intelligence will not countenance efforts to remove him. Within the limits of this system of protection, he operates with great freedom and daring, intervening far beyond the confines of the Arab world, in Malta and Ireland, in the Philippines and Uganda, and in many other places as well.

But the international poker game he plays so **dashingly** is perilous. If he steps beyond the limits

laid down by his protectors, he risks being cut down.
His ambition is not only to unite with Egypt, but
eventually to rule both Egypt and Libya together.
Will the clever Egyptians allow it, or will they axe
him once he has brought union about? His dream is to
make war on Israel and force it to disgorge every last
acre. Will America be so keen to defend him if
Armageddon ever gets beyond a gleam in his eye?
Without a doubt, if Qadhafi attacks a really vital
interest of America, Israel or Egypt, his days will be
counted. But in the meantime, by his acts, words and
ideas, he is daily enlarging his following among the
Arab masses. In the poker game this is Qadhafi's best
card, the hope that one day his popularity will be so
great that he will be able to defy even his protectors.

So far that day has not come. When the Hilton
assignment was reaching its climax in the early spring
of 1971, many people still thought it their business to
look after Qadhafi. In hoping that America would be
indifferent to their assault, and Britain secretly glad
of its success, Umar al-Shalhi and James Kent had
discounted or underestimated some of the more
arcane factors in this complex equation, which at that
time were only just developing.

How you see a situation depends on where you are
standing. There were, and still are, many different
points of view on Qadhafi's rule in Libya. Shalhi
simply wanted his country back, the mercenaries
were risking their necks in what they conceived as a
pro-Western cause, the Egyptians defending their
union hopes, the Italians promoting their influence in
the Mediterranean, the British avoiding a backlash
whilst raising their hats to more powerful allies, the

Americans, as befits a super-power, pursuing their grand design.

It was no accident that two weeks after the impounding of Conquistador XIII at Trieste, President Nixon should, on 11 April 1971, send a message to Colonel Qadhafi expressing the hope of a friendship between their two countries.

16 The Moroccan Assassin

Early in April 1971 two Americans booked in at the Frankfurt Airport Hotel, the scene ten days earlier of Shalhi's champagne wake. Since that dismal day the three principal mourners had scattered in search of rest, real rest to soothe their jangled nerves. The long drawn out, finally abortive affair had driven them to the edge of exhaustion. Shalhi subjected himself to the expensively Spartan discipline of a Swiss health clinic, gave up drinking and smoking, and reduced his weight by over thirty pounds. James Kent retreated to the relaxation of spring on the Mediterranean, while William, casting off the wearisome burden of clandestinity, took off for a holiday in the Black Forest. The day after he returned to Frankfurt on 3 April, he learned at the hotel that someone was making inquiries about him—alarming information which promptly drove him out again.

The two Americans were clumsy. With hamhanded menace they first approached the girl in charge of the lobby shop in the hotel to ask if she knew William's movements, then tackled the concierge and the barman, and finally on a transparent excuse asked a chambermaid for the key to his room. William had stayed a lot at the Airport Hotel and was well known to the staff there, many of them Italians with whom William, speaking their language fluently, was on excellent terms. So the Americans were met with a frosty response. The chambermaid went straight to the manager, German security officials were immediately called in, and the Americans summarily hustled off the premises.

They were gone when William came back, to be questioned politely by the police in his turn. He explained that he was an émigré from Libya and that the Americans were doubtless interested in his political activities. What he did not tell the police was his suspicion that his visitors were professional hit-men, sent to silence him by Yassin Ubaid's office in Rome, a European base for Libyan intelligence. To Shalhi and Kent, when they met William to review their prospects two weeks later, it seemed ominously clear that the Libyans had picked up their trail. Was this a revival of the counterplot? Or was it a fresh offensive mounted against them from Tripoli on a detailed brief prepared and handed over to the Libyans by a Western intelligence service? Their tracks over the past six months were too muddied and confused for them to trace the source of the leak with any certainty.

Whatever the truth, this incident with its undertone of physical violence was enough to bring home to them that their enemies were as determined as they were themselves. They could not forget that the Algerian opposition leader Belqasim Krim had been found strangled in the Frankfurt Intercontinental on 20 October 1970. A week before his death he had met Shalhi to ask whether, if Shalhi returned to power, Krim's guerrillas could have facilities to attack Algeria from Libyan bases. Was it now Shalhi's turn to be hunted down?

Until the scuppering of the Hilton assignment at Trieste, they had been able to persuade themselves that the great powers might be indifferent to their plans. Now they realised they would face the active hostility not only of Libya but of Britain, Italy and the United States. The dimensions of the problem had changed. The basic idea of a strike against the Tripoli jail was still good, but to continue with it would require a far more sophisticated level of security and the mobilisation of far greater resources. The operation could no longer be mounted in space. To take on governments needed a firm base and the backing of a government. To take on Qadhafi and his protectors in this new dimension, a state and a ruler were required who disliked him as much as Shalhi did.

It was three months before Shalhi found one.

But first the debris of failure had to be cleared up. The dramatic swoop on Conquistador on 21 March had left many things to be sorted out, the captain and Jock Fraser in prison and Léon, Jules and their men in Tangier. It was Kent's dismal task to straighten out all the tangles, not this time as the inquisitor but as the steward of Shalhi's costly investment.

One nasty problem was the equipment which the Italian police had found on board the sequestered boat. None of it was strictly speaking warlike, but taken together it betrayed warlike intentions. There were sheath-knives, ammunition pouches, water

A ma prise de fonction ▮▮▮▮ ▮▮▮▮▮▮▮▮▮▮▮▮▮▮▮▮. j'ai constaté des traces de sabotage sur le moteur. Tel notamment. de la limaille de fer et de bronze du genre copeaux de Fraiseuses et de Tour dans le remplissage d'huile ainsi que sur les culbuteurs du cylindre N° 4. - J'ai découvert également des traces de cette même limaille dans le filtre à huile du carter des engrenages; ce qui a certainement contribué au mauvais fonctionnement de l'embrayage j'attire l'attention des dégats que cette limaille aurait pu produire si elle était passée dans le circuit de graissage

le mécanicien.

▮▮▮▮▮▮▮▮▮▮▮▮▮▮▮▮▮▮▮▮▮▮

▮▮▮▮▮▮▮▮▮▮▮▮▮▮▮▮▮▮▮▮▮▮

Report on the sabotage of the Conquistador

bottles, webbing belts, great quantities of sacks and
kitbags, and two illustrated catalogues of small arms.
There were also wire-cutters and wire-cutting gloves,
reels of electric wiring, twine and adhesive tape,
diagrams of electric circuits and, more compromis-
ingly, fourteen fuses, ten detonators and two electric
initiation sets. To a practised eye, here were the
accessories of an arsenal: only the weapons, ammunition and explosives were missing.

The fuses and detonators were a mystery to Kent.
They should certainly not have been on board, as a
full supply was waiting with the rest of the explosives
at Ploče. Either someone had disobeyed orders or the
Italians had planted them on the ship to give
themselves a pretext for arresting Fraser and the
captain. The truth was never established. But it was
on a charge of the illegal presence on the boat of
fuses and detonators that the captain and Fraser were
held.

It took the Italian police little time to establish
that the captain had newly joined the ship and knew
nothing about her curious cargo. He was released and
despatched to France with the crew. Fraser was kept
in jail for four days, then released one evening, taken
to his hotel and told to stay there, and at 5.30 the
next morning was bundled from his bed and put on a
plane for London. He asked for a flight to Geneva,
but the carabinieri were adamant—he was British, and
on the first flight to Britain he would go.

When the case came before the Trieste court a month
later, he was convicted and given a suspended
sentence of four months' imprisonment and a 40,000
lire (about sixty dollars) fine. This meant that he

would not have to pay or go to prison unless he were convicted in Italy for another offence within the next five years. In the view of the Italian lawyer handling the case, the sentence had been passed to save the police's face, and he pressed to be allowed to appeal. Whoever mobilised the carabinieri from Rome was less interested in the punishment of Fraser than in the stalling of Shalhi.

Now to get Conquistador home. Kent, from a temporary headquarters in the Ritz Hotel, Paris, sent a French captain and crew of three to Trieste to make contact with the lawyer and take over the ship. The captain's orders were to sail the ship back around Italy to the small French Mediterranean port of Sète. This was easier said than done. When the ship's engineer came to check the two Mercedes engines, he discovered that one had been sabotaged: someone had emptied a load of iron filings into one of the cylinder blocks. Conquistador limped back to France on one engine.

She could be of no further use to the Hilton assignment. Bitterly Kent reflected that a more pedestrian looking vessel, even if much slower, would have suited their purpose better. In the end Conquistador, having cost Shalhi upwards of 100,000 dollars, was sold for scrap for a mere six thousand. Unless someone is mounting a military operation, there is little demand for that kind of boat.

In settling affairs Kent had more than once to dismiss his mercenary friends' suggestions of illegal solutions. One proposal was for Conquistador to have an 'accident' at sea, leaving the insurance to be claimed. Another was to recover some of the outlay on the arms, and particularly the explosives, by selling them to the IRA whose purchasing agents in Paris were not hard to find. An Irishman could make the right sort of contacts in the French capital without much difficulty, even in the government machine, where many die-hard gaullist officials had no love for the British. In the event the fifty-five crates were left in the warehouse at Ploče, and arrangements were made with the Yugoslavs for the three-month transit permit to be extended.

The return of Léon's disgruntled team from Tangier immediately after the seizure of Conquistador had not been entirely uneventful. Several had crossed by ferry to Algeciras and then travelled by train to Paris, but there was one casualty. On landing in Spain the mercenaries were searched by customs officials and one was found to be carrying a revolver, which was enough to put him in prison at Malaga until Kent could arrange to buy him out for 50,000 pesetas, Léon, driven out of France in the middle 1960s by de Gaulle's crack-down on the OAS, had taken refuge for a time in Spain where he had made useful friends in the Falange. Even so, it took ten days to free the mercenary. He had disobeyed orders: Kent's firm ruling was that the team had to travel clean, carrying no weapons.

By this time it was judged that the mercenaries had had enough. After three false starts their zeal and courage had leaked away, probably beyond salvaging. The odds of success had shortened to the point where even the least imaginative would foresee a hostile welcome on arrival at the target. Kent was not sorry to see the last of them. Léon and Jules had given sterling service, but security had been too endangered for them or their team to be of further use.

This was made dramatically plain by a message Kent received from the French mercenary commander Roger Faulques, an experienced and respected leader. Faulques, a former officer in the Foreign Legion, had collected scars from campaigns in Indo-China, Algeria, the Congo, Yemen and Biafra. The message from Faulques which reached Kent was simply, 'I don't think much of the team you have. Why not use me?'

It was time for the pay-off. Returning from the Riviera, Kent arranged to meet Jock Fraser, Léon and Jules at Geneva on Wednesday, 7 April 1971. Almost for the last time he drew from William several thousands of dollars in hundred-dollar bills, to cover the final payments and expenses. Fraser took his money and went. Jules then arrived by road from Paris, but alone. Because of a passport difficulty Léon had been turned back at the Swiss frontier, and Kent had to drive into France to hand over the roll of dollar bills.

For Kent too the end of the line was in sight. For nine months he had lived, breathed, dreamed the Hilton assignment, bearing the brunt of the reverses of fortune and never sparing himself. He had done his professional best and suffered no shame for the defeat. But the contest had moved to a level where to pursue further a 'private initiative' would only be quixotic. It was time for him to hand over his responsibilities and bow out.

This was not going to be easy, for Shalhi was far

from ready to throw in the sponge. So much became
clear when Shalhi, Kent and William met in Germany
in May 1971 for a long post mortem. The principal
displayed a good deal of robustness. He would not
just let the plan die of inertia. Back in fighting form
after his spell in the clinic, he was determined to
explore new ways of getting at Qadhafi. Someone,
somewhere in the world, could help him succeed.
Nobody could now accuse him of betraying his sacred
duty to his former patron King Idris: honour at least
was satisfied. But he still wanted to win.

As the spring turned into summer, Shalhi tenta-
tively canvassed for support in the Arab world. He
tried the oil-rich shaikhdoms of the Persian Gulf, the
kingdom of Saudi Arabia, King Hussain of Jordan
(whose murder Qadhafi had publicly called for). Oil
companies were considered and he explored yet again
the ranks of political exiles. He was met with
sympathy but little else.

Then, on 10 July 1971, an attempt was made on
the life of King Hasan of Morocco. The king was by
the sea at Skhirat celebrating his forty-second birthday with several hundred guests, including most of
the foreign ambassadors and their senior staffs, when
the 1,400 officer cadets from the Ahermoumou
military school surrounded the palace and opened fire
with rockets and machine guns. Ninety-two people
were officially reported to have been killed and 133
injured. But Hasan miraculously survived, and with
great presence of mind turned the tables on the
insurgents, giving his trusted henchman General
Muhammad Oufkir total authority to put down the
revolt and stamp out the pockets of rebellion in the

armed forces. Within an hour of the attack on King Hasan Radio Libya was joyfully on the air, in the belief that the rebels had triumphed. On Qadhafi's orders, messages of support for the rebels were broadcast and promises that Libya's 'shock forces, paratroopers, bombers and huge troop carriers' were preparing to fly to the aid of the Moroccan people.

Shalhi had found the base he wanted.

Less than a month after the attempted Moroccan coup, when Morocco had broken off relations with Libya and when Oufkir was busy executing generals and other ringleaders, Shalhi through Arab intermediaries made contact with Hasan and was invited to Rabat. The king instructed Oufkir to give him all necessary assistance.

It needed only one brief meeting for Shalhi and the Moroccan strong man to establish agreement in principle to overthrow Qadhafi and his regime. Oufkir, a professional soldier who had distinguished himself not only by his total ruthlessness in the king's cause but also, earlier, as a much decorated officer in the French army in Indo-China, wanted to know what assets Shalhi could mobilise within Libya, what men, arms and funds he had at his disposal, what operational plans he had made. It was decided that James Kent should visit Morocco to brief General Oufkir and shift the burdens of the Hilton assignment from his own shoulders to the broader ones of the Moroccan state.

The Rabat Hilton was like a graveyard when Kent arrived with a woman assistant Jane Spencer early in September. Two months after the attempt on Hasan, the Moroccan capital was still in the grip of crisis as

General Mohammad Oufkir (Associated Press)

Oufkir's merciless purge proceeded. Tourists had been frightened away.

General Oufkir too was away, impressing his forceful personality on the country, zig-zagging from one military unit to another, showing himself to troops and populace, confronting wavering officers, despatching men to their death. It seemed to Kent that Oufkir was as feverishly mobile as he himself had been in Europe. This was what the Moroccan situation demanded: there was no authority stronger than the personality behind it, no solution except physical presence. So Kent and Jane Spencer sunbathed by the pool in the Hilton, waiting to be called.

Five days later, just as Kent was dressing for dinner, the call came. A car was being sent to take them to the general—at Fez, some three-and-a-half hours' drive away. Oufkir was dining with senior officers and civic dignitaries at the Holiday Inn when Kent and Jane Spencer arrived just before midnight. Taken to meet the general in a private room, Kent was told by Oufkir that he could have a short talk there and then, or preferably a longer discussion in the morning. Kent saw the general would prefer to wait until the morning.

It was the wrong choice. When Kent got up next day he learned that Oufkir had been forced to change his plans, was about to depart for Tangier and wanted the English couple to follow him there. He had arranged a car and driver, an orderly and accommodation at the Rif Hotel, where he would make contact. Oufkir then rushed off in a cavalcade of vehicles, followed a little later by Kent and his assistant. But they were no luckier in Tangier. After a day of

hanging about within reach of the telephone, they
were summoned back to Rabat at speed by Oufkir's
apologetic aide-de-camp. Back into the car, across
northern Morocco by night, and into the Hilton
again. The next day the aide was on the line, more
apologetic then ever: the general had had to fly
south, to deal with problems near Marrakesh. Kent
began to feel he was appearing in a Keystone cops
movie, but he was not resentful: he could understand
Oufkir's need for intense activity and rapid movement. But his own affairs were pressing in Europe,
and Jane Spencer had to be despatched to look after
them.

At last the much deferred meeting took place in
Oufkir's home in Rabat. The general had just come in
by helicopter from the south and had changed into
tan slacks and a pink shirt. A tall, commanding,
rather hawk-like figure, he looked very much the
lean, hard, well-to-do man one might see on the
Riviera.

When Shalhi had met Oufkir a month earlier, he
had spoken only in general terms of a planned strike
against Libya. Kent thought it time to explain to the
Moroccan the precise details of the operation, and
outlined to him the elegantly simple lines of the
mercenary assault on the jail. Oufkir's enthusiasm was
immediately fired. 'Where are the army barracks?' he
demanded, poring over Kent's diagrams. 'Which are
the approach roads? I think your diversion groups
need reinforcing.' Kent told him of the arms and
explosives waiting at Ploče, and of a new mercenary
team recruited principally in Belgium and Luxembourg—a standby team which Kent had himself

mustered some months earlier, unknown to anyone but Shalhi and William, as an insurance against the withdrawal of Léon and the French. Ships were no problem: they could be acquired when necessary. Shalhi had spent a great deal of money but he was not yet at the end of his resources. What was most needed was a secure base from which an assault force could be launched against its target.

Oufkir agreed that the Hilton assignment could work. But he asked, 'Why attack the prison? Why not assassinate Qadhafi?' Kent explained that neither he nor Shalhi believed in assassination. Anyway it was tactically difficult, as Qadhafi rarely moved beyond Libya and Egypt where he was extremely well guarded. Moreover, it tended to be counter-productive. It might destroy the man but not necessarily the regime, and it would not be well received or arouse much sympathy or support in the world. The Moroccan shook his head. It was quite clear that he thoroughly believed in assassination, and that he was studying one or two plans of his own on these lines.

In the middle of this callous conversation the telephone rang. It was Oufkir's wife, calling from Madrid. Almost without changing gear, the general switched from talking murder to tender inquiries about her health. And then back to murder.

After two hours of discussion, Oufkir agreed to provide Shalhi with a base in Morocco and personally to take over the military co-ordination. Confident that the Egyptian garrisons in Libya would turn and run at the first sound of gunfire, he spoke of strengthening or replacing the mercenary force with his own Moroccan commandos, and of widening Shalhi's plan to make sure that Qadhafi did not escape the strike.

Next morning, on Oufkir's instructions, a colonel, one of Oufkir's military assistants, collected Kent at 6.45 and flew him in a light aircraft to the airfield near Al Husaima, a small port a hundred kilometres east of Tangier. Kent was given authority to inspect the harbour and make arrangements with the port commandant for the reception and storage of the arms and explosives. He noted the chalets of the nearby Club Méditerranée—they could provide useful cover for European mercenaries moving in and out of the area.

In different circumstances, and if he had been a different man, Kent might have enjoyed a holiday at the Club himself. Now he was glad to be going away, leaving someone else in charge.

There was only one thing left to do—deliver the weapons and explosives to Oufkir. The crates in Yugoslavia had outrun their extended transit permit, and Kent had once again to call upon Gregor Jirasek's services to arrange their release from the warehouse. Early in October 1971 a ship was chartered to move the cargo from Ploče to Al Husaima, an uneventful voyage. The consignment was taken over by the Moroccan military authorities and stored at a camp some five miles inland from the harbour.

Shalhi waited, and kept in touch.

But before General Oufkir could turn his fire on Qadhafi, he had some domestic problems to settle. The man who for so long had been the chief support of the Moroccan throne, master of the murderous intrigues at court, ferocious scourge of the king's enemies, now coveted his sovereign's place. King Hasan was the only obstacle to supreme power and, with the killer's instinct, Oufkir planned to slay the king and rule Morocco in his stead—or so the king would today have us believe.

Oufkir planned a perfect crime, an accident to the king's plane over the sea, leaving no trace. On 16 August 1972 three Moroccan airforce F-5s opened fire on King Hasan's Boeing 727 jetliner over the Mediterranean. On board were Hasan, three of his children and his only brother Prince Moulay Abdullah. All survived thanks to the king's quick thinking. With great coolness he took command of the situation, ordering the pilot to land and himself taking over radio and announcing that the king had been hit and others seriously wounded. This ploy deceived the plotters.

The king regained control, but Oufkir died at the palace that night. Hasan said it was suicide, but Oufkir's bullet-riddled corpse suggested otherwise. Some people believe that Hasan himself gunned down his savage watchdog.

The interesting details came later. Ten days after his escape the king gave a press conference to persuade the world of General Oufkir's infamy. He related that when the jets opened fire on his plane, a conversation with Oufkir flashed across his mind 'immediately, just like a film.'

It has taken place the previous winter when Oufkir was reporting to the king about an official visit Colonel Qadhafi of Libya was due to make to Mauretania. He would have to overfly the Sahara. 'If we could find out Qadhafi's flight plan,' Oufkir said, 'what would you think of sending an F-5 to smash him into the middle of the desert?' 'Oufkir, are you mad?' Hasan claims to have replied. 'Even supposing we knew his flight plan, his altitude, his route, and we hit him, you must realise that there would be an inquiry. They would find traces of bullets and rockets. In this area only Morocco has F-5s. Can you imagine the international scandal? Piracy in mid-air against a chief of state?'

In this roundabout way, and posthumously, was Oufkir's thinking about Qadhafi's removal revealed. Assassination appears to have tempted him more than the release of prisoners from the Hilton. But he died before either plan could be attempted.

BILL OF LADING No.2

UNIFORM BILL OF LADING 1946

approved by

The Documentary council of The Baltic and International Maritime Conference.

To be used with Charter — Parties.

Code Name: Congenbill.

SHIPPED at **P L O Č E**
in apparent good order and condition by **"INTEREUROPA"**
of **RIJEKA** on board the good Vessel called the ▮▮▮▮▮▮
for carriage to **EL HOSEIMA /MAROKO/ FOR TRANSHIPMENT TO DUALA**
or so near thereto as she may safely get, following goods:

MARKS

37-0-103
FORT LAMY
1-52

52 **CASSES INFANTRY ARMS &**   **2.800 Kgs**
    ═══════ AMMUNITION   **══════════**

"ON BOARD"

NOTIFY: ▮▮▮▮▮▮▮▮▮▮▮▮▮▮▮▮ **FORT LAMY — CHAD**

FREIGHT PAYABLE AS PER AGREEMENT

(of which   on deck at Shippers' risk; the Carrier not being responsible
for loss or damage howsoever arising) which are to be delivered in the like good order and
condition at the aforesaid Port of **EL HOSEIMA /MAROKO/ FOR TRANSHIPMENT TO**to
DUALA   T O   O R D E R
or his or their Assign(s), he or they paying freight at the rate of
(say   per   ) as per Charter-Party, dated
All the terms, conditions, liberties, and exceptions of the Charter- Party are herewith
incorporated.

This Bill of Lading shall have effect subject of the provisions of any legislation relating to the carriage of goods by sea which incorporates the rules relating to Bills of Lading contained in the international Convention, dated Brussels 25th August, 1924 and which is compulsorily applicable to the contract of carriage herein contained. Such legislation shall be deemed to be incorporated herein, but nothing herein contained shall be deemed a surrender by the Carrier of any of its rights or immunities or an increase of any of its responsibilities or liabilities thereunder. If any term of this Bill of Lading be repugnant to any extent to any legislation by this clause incorporated, such term shall be void to that extent but no further. Nothing in this Bill of Lading shall operate to limit or deprive the Carrier of any statutory protection or exemption from, or limitation of, liability.

Freight Advance.
Received on account
of freight:

Weight, measure, quality, quantity, condition, contents and value unknown..

IN WITNESS whereof the Master or Agent of the said Vessel has signed **Three**
Bills of Lading all of this tenor and date, any one of which being accomplished the others
to be void.   **Ploče,** the **14.10.** 19 **71**

MASTER :

Epilogue

You can do a lot with Diners Club, Hertz cars and an adequate supply of hundred-dollar bills: you can even run a military operation. But if it is to succeed a 'private initiative' needs more than money, more than skill and ingenuity. It needs luck, a favourable international context, and speed. If an operation is carried through fast enough, it stands a good chance of getting past the guard of the world's secret services, even the omniscient CIA. Government agencies are by their very nature lumbering, particularly when they are under firm political control as in Britain. The Hilton assignment missed its moment. It was an operation which overran itself, giving its opponents time to mobilise their will and resources against it.

But future activists should beware. The growth of international terrorism has driven many governments greatly to expand their secret security forces. The climate for private armies is bleak.

Umar al-Shalhi lost his round against Qadhafi, but has he lost the war? Shalhi has retired behind the electronic devices of his Geneva villa. But Arab politics are volatile. It would need only a small shift in the power balance—a change of regime in Egypt, a resurgence of Libyan nationalism against an Egyptian takeover, a direct clash between Qadhafi and Israel, a threat to America's oil interests in Libya, a change in America's grand design—for the colonel to be stripped of his protectors and look vulnerable again. Shalhi has no alternative but to play a waiting game.

There is a chance that, given enough rope, the Libyan leader will hang himself. Qadhafi is an ambitious young man with an interest in history. He has read biographies of Napoleon and is not unaware that the man who became Emperor of France and master of Europe started humbly in Corsica. Libya, another backwater, could provide a leader for all the Arabs. In pressing for union with Egypt, Qadhafi dreams of assuming Nasser's mantle. He is heading into a storm, but at the time of writing he prospers, daily richer and more influential.

King Idris, the man he overthrew, continues to live in pious, modest retirement in a large villa in suburban Cairo, remote from the political fray. Equally passive, Abd al-Aziz al-Shalhi and some 150 others remain unwilling guests of the Tripoli 'Hilton.'

Life has been relatively kind to the other actors in the drama. Colonel David Stirling runs his business enterprises from an address in Mayfair and lives nearby. James Kent has moved his base abroad to a more congenial climate. William has given up dangerous politics and started an import-export business in West Germany. Jeff Thompson, the ex-British warrant officer, is in distant Arabia helping to train the army of a local ruler. John Brooke Miller has aspirations in the property business.

The South African Steve Reynolds has returned to commerce, while his secretary Tracey now lives in Australia. The bluff arms contact man, Frank Higgins, is now married to his girl-friend Louise and was last heard of in Rabat. Gregor Jirasek and Stefan Vlček continue to provide useful services for Western businessmen trading in Central Europe.

The ever resourceful Léon has installed a row of vending machines to sell snacks and drinks to truck drivers at the new Paris wholesale food market off the autoroute to Orly. It is a tough milieu which Léon can well cope with. But Annette complains that she has to get up at five in the morning to cut and pack the sandwiches.

TRIPOLI The target

GENEVA Home of the Arab paymaster

PARIS Where the mercenaries were recruited

PRAGUE Where the arms and explosives were bought

DUBROVNIK A lost arms cargo

PLOČE Licensed to export explosives

BARI Disaster port

ROME Counterplotters' HQ

TOULON Conquistador's home port

NAPLES Operational HQ, stage 2

FRANKFURT Operational HQ, stage 3

TUNIS Where a mercenary lost his nerve

TRIESTE The end of the line

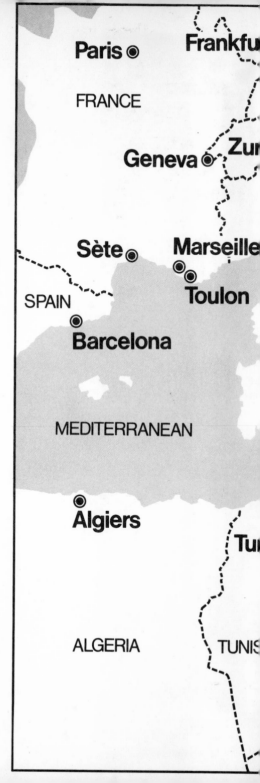